A DROP IN THE OCEAN

A DROP IN THE OCEAN

◆

DRAMATIC ACCOUNTS OF AIRCREW SAVED FROM THE SEA

by

Jim Burtt–Smith

John French

LEO COOPER

LONDON

First published in Great Britain in 1996 by
LEO COOPER
190 Shaftesbury Avenue, London WC2H 8JL
an imprint of
Pen & Sword Books Ltd,
47 Church Street,
Barnsley, South Yorkshire S70 2AS

A CIP record for this book is available from the British Library

ISBN 0 85052 5071 1

Typeset by Phoenix Typesetting,
Ilkley, West Yorkshire.

Printed in Great Britain by Redwood Books Ltd,
Trowbridge, Wilts.

CONTENTS

ACKNOWLEDGEMENTS

The authors are happy to acknowledge the help they have received from the Goldfish who have contributed their stories, and from the Goldfish Club and its Newsletter Editor, Geoff Copeman, for permission to use extracts from their publications. They apologize for the omission of a few photographs which were found to be technically unsuitable for reproduction.

PREFACE

The following stories were collected by Jim Burtt-Smith, author of *One of the Many on the Move* and the Goldfish Club Chairman, and edited by John French, former Club secretary. The stories highlight the magnificent and dedicated efforts of the Marine Section of the R.A.F. Air Sea Rescue, whose crews bore to safety their air crew colleagues who had 'ditched'.

It is hoped they will convey some sense of the trauma and fears of those who crashed into the sea and were tossed about on twenty- or thirty-foot waves in freezing cold weather. This they endured, shocked and stressed, seasick, sometimes for days on end. Then in the distance they would hear a faint noise, becoming louder and louder, until out of the mist roared an ASR High Speed Launch, powered by its three Napier Lion engines. Willing hands dragged them aboard before the boat sped away at 35 or 40 knots, returning to base with the gunners keeping watch for the enemy.

Although this book deals with the RAF rescuers and is dedicated to those brave men, tribute must also be paid to the fishermen, mostly Danish, and to the German Luftwaffe. Animosity was forgotten in those traumatic hours.

The authors' sincere thanks are extended to Les Bartlett, who supplied the information about the ASR Service, and also to Ken Rimell and all former HSL crew members who contributed to this book.

INTRODUCTION

These are recollections of a few of the 9,000 airmen whose lives were saved firstly by their 'Mae Wests' and secondly by their dinghies. Half of them were plucked from the sea by the RAF Air Sea Rescue Service; the crews set out night and day, often in atrocious weather, to pick up their comrades who, without such dedication, would surely have perished.

The welcoming roar of the three Napier engines of the ASR launches was music to the ears of 'ditched' aircrews, who were usually treated to a tot of rum, hot cocoa and a covering of warm blankets.

One such rescue was accomplished after a running battle against a German E-boat, which was just pipped at the post.

In another incident, the crew of a Lancaster died one by one in the dinghy and their bodies were slipped over the side by the sole survivor: he was found, after eleven days, by a German air sea rescue boat which had been following the trail of corpses.

Our ASR service picked up anyone of any nationality who had ditched, as did the Germans.

We who are still alive give our heartfelt thanks to the brave men of the ASR Service who rescued us from the sea and gave us, perhaps, another fifty years of life.

The 9,000 aircrew who ditched were originally members of the world's most exclusive club, the Goldfish Club; fifty years after the end of the Second World War the Club is still very active, although membership has dwindled to about 600 worldwide.

Jim Burtt-Smith
J. O. French

THE CHARLES HARRISON STORY:
A Wet Whitley

Charles Harrison's first encounter with the sea was on 12 June, 1941, when he flew in a Whitley Mark 5 with 10 Squadron from Leeming in Yorkshire. The target was Schwerte in the Ruhr. Charles was filling in as tail gunner with a crew whose normal gunner was ill. Here is his story.

'Just after passing over the Dutch coast we ran into some light, sporadic flak, which was close. Several minutes later I saw a mass of sparks fly past my turret from the starboard engine. There followed some conversation on the intercom between the crew about the state of the engine. It was decided that we should drop our bombs in the sea and turn back: in the meantime, the starboard engine was feathered.

'Shortly afterwards the pilot called me and said he was having difficulty in maintaining height. He asked me to leave the turret, go into the fuselage and get rid of all the loose and heavy stuff I could find.

'After disconnecting my intercom lead I opened the fuselage door to jettison some incendiary bombs and flares, and I remember saying to myself, "Hell, that sea looks close!" I threw out all I could find when I felt a tugging on my arm. It was the wireless operator, who shouted, "Go back to the turret – the skipper wants you." I returned to the turret and plugged in the intercom. The pilot told me he could no longer maintain height and there was a "possibility" that we would have to land in the sea. He asked me to go back to the fuselage and prepare the dinghy for launching.

'In the Whitley the dinghy was opposite the fuselage door and secured to the starboard side wall by "bungee" cords. Once again

I opened my turret door, disconnected the i/c and went to grab the two handles to hoist myself out of the turret.

'In the next seconds I was aware of an impact on the back of my head, a flash of light and stars behind my eyes. When I regained my senses I was lying in water in the fuselage. Everything was dark and quiet. On operations I always carried a torch stowed in my flying boot and I shone the torch into the darkness. I then saw that I was down the fuselage by the door, having been thrown backwards from the turret. In the process I had cleared the spar which supported the tail wheel and lay across the fuselage, about two feet high, from one side to the other.

'My next thoughts were "The door – and the dinghy". I freed the dinghy and opened the fuselage door to throw it out, retaining hold of the lanyard in order to inflate it when it hit the sea.

'Then the wireless operator appeared. He had come out of the top hatch and crawled along the fuselage to the outside of the door. As I threw out the dinghy and pulled the lanyard he put his hand underneath to help it out, but his action turned the dinghy pack over and it inflated upside down. Before anything could be done the rest of the crew were in it. I had to swim for it and was last man in. It was about two in the morning, pitch dark, and we paddled hard to get away from the Whitley, which disappeared beneath the waves in less than two minutes. The navigator had injured himself in the impact; my neck and head ached, but I think I escaped serious injury due to my flying helmet and my para-suit. There had been no warning from the pilot and the crash into the water had been quite sudden. There was a heavy swell. We discussed the possibility of getting out and trying to right the dinghy when daylight came, but the navigator, apart from his injury, could not swim. So we agreed to manage with the upturned dinghy, although this meant no accessibility to all the aids normally carried in the dinghy.

'We heard our own planes returning home from the raid and also some enemy planes returning from Britain. There was great satisfaction when dawn broke and, as the wireless operator had sent out an SOS before we ditched, we hoped for an early rescue.

'After a time what appeared to be a launch was sighted in the distance, but it was not heading towards us and eventually disappeared over the horizon. Then came the sound of an aircraft and we saw a German plane flying quite low. It was a seaplane and the pilot was clearly visible. We began waving to him. He waved back, but we assumed he had been searching for German aircraft. As he circled low above us, he fired two Very lights and then flew off in the direction in which we had seen the launch. Minutes later more Very lights lit the sky. The German pilot reappeared, circled us and fired two more Very lights before disappearing. We settled down and tried to accept the fact that we were about to be picked up by the enemy.

'Not long after, we spotted two planes diving and circling as though engaged in a dog fight. They seemed to be Hurricanes or Spitfires. One of them suddenly dived and flew right over the dinghy. It was a Spitfire and the pilot was waving to us. His colleague had gone, presumably to fetch help. As the fighter continued to circle overhead, the boat we had seen earlier was now approaching fast. We recognised it as an A.S.R. launch – an ocean-going type with four gun turrets fore and aft.

'All of us, and the dinghy, were pulled aboard and taken below to a comfortable cabin with beds. The skipper told us that they had been searching for us when a German plane approached and fired signal flares. The crew immediately radioed Great Yarmouth for a fighter escort, fully expecting to be attacked. All turrets in the launch were manned. They certainly did not realize that the enemy pilot was merely trying to attract the launch to our position. It was, however, one of the escort fighters which eventually sighted the dinghy and brought the rescue launch to our position, just as they were about to return to port. We had been in the dinghy for eight-and-a-half hours.

'After we had each swallowed a large glass of Naval rum no one seemed to be able to remember anything more until the launch tied up at the A.S.R. station in Great Yarmouth. The rest of that day and the following night were spent in a Seamen's Hospital, but we were kept awake by the sound of bombs dropping in and around Great Yarmouth. Next morning our Commanding Officer sent his vehicle to take us back to Leeming. Meanwhile the Yarmouth ASR had kitted us out in basic Naval uniform in place of our own sodden clothing.

'There was a strange welcome as we stopped at traffic lights in Yarmouth: members of the local population were swearing and hissing at us in the belief that we were captured German airmen from the previous night's raid. There was some surprise when the navigator lowered the window and told them, in very colourful English, who we really were.

'I was the only member of that crew who survived the war.'

Crew of Whitley:
P.O. Littlewood (pilot); Sgt Poupard (second pilot); P.O. Stevens-Fox (navigator); Sgt Wilkinson (wireless operator); Sgt Harrison (air gunner).

THE CHARLES HARRISON STORY:
First Dip For A Halifax

Ten months later, 10 Squadron at Leeming had been converted to Halifax bombers. The target on the night of 14/15 April, 1942, was Dortmund, but to Charles Harrison there was something strangely ominous about the operation even before his Halifax Mark 2 was airborne. They were to carry two 4,000 pound bombs – the first time for a Halifax – and since the bomb doors had not been modified they could not be properly closed and would create a drag on the aircraft. Moreover, they were given the longest possible route to the target in order to attack Dortmund from an easterly direction. Finally, the excess weight being carried demanded that the two outer wing petrol tanks be left empty. No encouragement here for a bomber crew setting off for the heart of enemy territory.

Let Charles Harrison continue the story.

'The flight outward was quiet and uneventful and we were unaffected by flak or searchlights. Some time before reaching the target, however, I heard the flight engineer tell the skipper that we had already used just over half of our petrol. Heavy cloud was building up and after our attack on Dortmund it got worse. Our final turning point was a lake south of the Ruhr Valley. From there our track took us back the way we had come. After sighting the lake and changing course we flew on dead reckoning through the heavy cloud.

'All went well until the point at which we should have crossed the coast, but it was still impossible to see the ground. The skipper remarked about the fuel running low and I was asked by the navigator to get a radio fix. Our normal M/F stations, dotted along the east coast, could not pinpoint us for a fix, but gave us a line bearing. This indicated that we were a long way south of our intended

17

position. I succeeded in getting a fix from three other M/F stations on the south coast. They placed us over the Channel Islands. The skipper estimated he had no more than ten or twenty minutes' fuel left and told me to begin transmitting an SOS. At that point the rear gunner sighted two islands through a break in the cloud. "And they're firing at us!"

'This clearly verified the fix and we immediately set course for the nearest English coast. We flew on, reducing height, with the Flight Engineer draining the tanks and, when necessary, cutting an engine. Suddenly there were searchlights ahead. We were approaching the coast.

'The pilot then gave the warning to ditch. At that point I decided we would not be caught out, as on the previous ditching, with no means of signalling. Accordingly I filled a parachute bag with cartridges, signal flares and a Very pistol, and asked the rest of the crew to pocket any other Very cartridges they could find. We were still on SOS procedure and the Morse key was clamped down. We remained at the front, while the navigator and wireless operator went back to the fuselage 'rest' position. Only one engine was still functioning when we hit the sea.

'Everyone went out quickly through the upper fuselage escape hatch. The dinghy was already nearly fully inflated on the port wing – sea water entering a grille on the nose began the automatic inflation process. The dinghy was launched, and as we all stepped in I held on tightly to my bag of rescue equipment.

'It was just getting light and we could make out high ground all around us, even seawards on both sides. We were actually in Lyme Bay, about four miles out from Seaton Harbour, which could clearly be seen as the light improved. As we set off cartridges and signal flares at frequent intervals, the dinghy drifted around the Halifax, which remained afloat. But we were heading seawards again.

'After about 2½ hours in the dinghy, a launch could be seen coming towards us from seawards. The first thought: is this a Jerry coming for us? Fortunately it was an ASR launch from Lyme Regis, about 8 miles distant around the headland.

'It was only a small launch, but we clambered aboard and sat near the stern in the open air. There was no room for the dinghy, so it was tied to the stern of the launch and towed, but a few minutes later it burst.

'All this time our Halifax had been floating well on top of the water. Having landed us at the Cobb, Lyme Regis, the ASR launch returned in an attempt to beach the aircraft but reached it just in time to watch it go under. It must have floated for about 3½ hours because of the empty fuel tanks.

'We changed out of our wet uniforms, after which the C.O. of Lyme Regis ASR, F/O Sir Algernon Guinness, Bart (one of the brewing family) took a photo of our crew. We stayed the rest of the day there and they told us we were the first bomber crew they had picked up.

'When evening arrived we were taken to Exeter airport, where a Bombay troop carrier took us, with another crew who had baled out just over the coast, to Hendon and thence back to Leeming.

'On our return we discovered that a hundred-mile-an-hour gale, not forecast by the meteorologists, had been responsible for blowing us right off course. This was also the first known Halifax ditching at night.'

One might imagine that two ditchings would have been quite enough excitement in the flying career of Charles Harrison. Not so. In October, 1942, six months after his second rescue by RAF ASR launch, he was forced to bale out of his aircraft near Bonn and spent the remaining two-and-a-half years of the war as a guest of the Third Reich.

PADDLING IN THE CHANNEL:
'Tiffies' To The Rescue

On 17 July, 1943, the following report appeared in the *Daily Express*:-

'Royal Air Force men told last night how, within sight of the French coast, fighters battled with twice their number of enemy planes to protect the crew of a "ditched" Wellington bomber.

'An airborne lifeboat was dropped by parachute to the Wellington men – six of them – and they were brought safely back to England. Two F.W. fighter-bombers were destroyed.

'The Wellington pilot is Wing Commander Norman A. Bray, of Shennington, near Banbury, Oxfordshire. This is what he said:-

> "We were hit by flak while returning from a raid and had to 'ditch' in the sea at about two o'clock on Wednesday morning. The aircraft filled with water immediately and we all went under, but managed to scramble out. Our 'ditching drill' was 100 per cent perfect. We had come down almost in the mouth of the Seine estuary, and once in the dinghy we had a battle against a current that threatened to carry us to the French coast, which we could see nearly all the time."

'Fighter Command planes sighted the dinghy on Thursday morning and flashed a signal to base. An Air-Sea Rescue Service plane carrying the lifeboat was sent out at once. It was escorted by 12 Typhoons.

'Fighter pilot Flying Officer Lloyd Wilson, an Australian, said:

> "We flew along the coast for about 20 minutes searching

for the dinghy. We sighted it about eight miles from shore. The men were paddling furiously to avoid drifting on to the coast. They looked slightly exhausted, but waved to us."

'The rescue plane pilot, Flying Officer W. Hender of New Zealand, released the lifeboat. Then the ditched airmen climbed out of their dinghy into the boat and soon had the engines going. They headed for England, 80 miles away, escorted by four Typhoons.

'The eight Typhoons left were circling low when double their number of F.W.190s were sighted. As the enemy prepared to dive to the attack the Typhoons' leader, Squadron Leader D. J. Scott, DFC and Bar, led his men to meet them, and they climbed to engage about 10 miles from the launch.

'One of the F.W.s destroyed was shared by the squadron leader and another pilot. In the fight Scott went into a spin several thousand feet up, recovering only when 500 feet above the water.

'But he saw his victim's parachute billowing out. The pilot who shot down the second F.W. said he saw only four of the 16 F.W.s "The one I got," he added, "was coming head-on, but turned, and after getting hits on him I followed and put in a few more bursts to make sure."

'Meanwhile, Air Sea Rescue high-speed launches had been ordered out from England to meet the lifeboat, and Fighter Command sent four squadrons of Spitfires to relieve the Typhoons, as it was thought that the enemy might attack in strength.

'An hour later more than 30 enemy aircraft appeared, but when they saw the Spitfires they made no attempt to fight but headed back for home.

'One of the launches intercepted the lifeboat and took the Wellington crew on board. On the way home it narrowly missed a mine. A second launch towed the lifeboat back to port.'

One of the Typhoon pilots, Desmond Scott, tells of the incident in his autobiography:-

'On 15 July we set out to complete the unfulfilled mission of the previous day, but we came across another bomber crew, this time British and far too close to Le Havre for comfort. I learned afterwards that this bomber crew had been in the water for several days. How the Germans had not sighted them is beyond comprehension.

'I left two sections, comprising four aircraft, over the dinghy and hurried back to Tangmere, for if ever there was a challenge this was it. I knew the reaction from HQ 11 Group would be for an international distress call to be sent out immediately, but I spoke to Air Vice-Marshal "Ding" Saunders and, although he was against it at first, he allowed me the responsibility of attempting a rescue. The Air Sea Rescue boys were soon on their way in a Hudson, under which was slung a special airborne lifeboat, and we made our rendezvous with them off the south coast. We escorted the Hudson to the dinghy, where I instructed the other two sections to return to Tangmere and refuel.

'The Hudson dropped its lifeboat which floated down on three huge parachutes. As it hit the sea, two covered areas in the stem and stern inflated automatically. These looked quite comfortable and well capable of transporting the six survivors back to safety. It appeared to have two outboard motors built into wells amidships, for soon after the crew had scrambled aboard I saw one of them starting up the motors. Within minutes they were cruising off on the 60-mile trip home.

'Everthing was going to plan, and as we circled low over our new charge the moles at Le Havre faded into the distance and the hot sun was making me feel sleepy. Suddenly I was brought up with a jolt when Jim McCaw cried out, "Sir! There are about a dozen bandits above you."

'I looked up and sure enough the duck-egg-blue bellies of a pack of Huns were circling directly above. They had the drop on us and I had the feeling normally associated with nakedness. But they did not seem keen to take the plunge. The others had returned from Tangmere by this time, so we made eight in all.

'I slowly circled away from the lifeboat and when we were well clear of it I instructed the boys to follow me and listen carefully for my command to "break". As soon as I straightened out, and we were more or less back in our pairs, the 109s and 190s pounced down on us. At the first sight of tracer I yelled out, "Break!" and swung up to port. I realized immediately that I had forgotten something when a 190 overshot and crossed to starboard right in front of me. I pressed the firing button, and as he flew through my fire I hit his slipstream and was thrown into a spin. Of all my close squeaks this must have been the closest, for in recovering I almost collected the pilot of the FW 190 as he was thrown from his aircraft a split second before the plane hit the sea. This spin-off was of my own making. While mentally mapping out my tactics I had forgotten to move my coarse cruising pitch into the fine position.

'I never saw any of my cannon shells hit this aircraft, although Fitz, in close attendance as usual, was sure they had. Jim McCaw, who was also near to me, said later that my prop missed hitting the water by inches. Pilot Officer Sames shot down an FW 190 and Spud Murphy and Umbers damaged another. Altogether we came out of it quite well. That night Lord Haw Haw, broadcasting from Berlin, announced that a furious air battle had been fought over the Channel near Le Havre. Well, it had not been all that big in terms of numbers, in fact quite small, but it had certainly been close for me.

'Air Sea Rescue launches met the lifeboat 30 miles off the coast and towed it into Newhaven. Wing Commander N. A. N. Bray, commander of the ditched Wellington and a friend of Paddy Crisham, insisted that 486 Squadron be given the lifeboat's centre-board, which we later turned into our official scoreboard. Two or three days later I received a moving letter from Bray, signed by each member of his crew. Written at the Navy sick quarters at Swanborough Manor near Lewes, where they were convalescing, it made me feel quite humble. Bray's salvation was all too short, as he was killed a few months later.'

PADDLING IN THE CHANNEL:
Bert Fitchett's Version

In moments of crisis strange thoughts may cross one's mind. Perhaps none could be more bizarre than those described by Bert Fitchett, who was the wireless operator on the Wellington which ditched on that day in July, 1943. Bert's report tells it all.

'As we slopped around in the dinghy I suddenly thought of the opening lines of Noel Coward's "Stately Homes of England", where a quartet of upper-class twits sing "Here we stand, the four of us, eldest sons who must succeed". It was a pretty poor analogy really, because for a start there were six of us crammed into that dinghy. And we were certainly not standing. Indeed, if any one of us had tried he would have been distinctly unpopular. Worst of all, unlike those "eldest sons", we were quite clearly not succeeding.
    'Our Wellington had been hit by a burst of flak over France when we were on our way to the target. The port engine was put out of action and the wing surfaces surrounding it were badly damaged, with the result that it was now impossible not only to reach our target, but also to reach England. Our skipper decided to abort and try to clear the French coast to ditch in the Channel. The bombs were jettisoned and eventually we came down safely in the Seine estuary at two o'clock in the morning on 14 July, 1943. We could see the lights of Le Havre, so we used paddles to counter the current that was threatening to take us inshore. By nine o'clock that morning we were still too close to Le Havre for comfort; a renewed effort with the paddles took us a little farther out. At about this time a lone Spitfire spotted us, circled twice and made off towards England. Despite this, no help came all that day, which we spent paddling incessantly to keep away from the French coast. By 0130 hours on the 15th the skipper ordered a rest for three

hours. The sea drogue was put out and we dozed, leaving two men on watch. Daylight came, the sun climbed steadily, but after 34 hours in the dinghy there was still no sign of rescue. We were cold, wet, weary and hungry. Not surprisingly, there was not much chat now. Each man was immersed in his own thoughts.

'I was musing on the fact that we were at least lucky to be alive, largely due to the sturdy nature of the Wellington's construction which had stood up so well to the impact and given the whole crew time to take to the dinghy. Clever chap, I thought, the engineer who designed that airframe, but he had almost certainly taken the concept from nature. For example, the honeycomb or the spider's web – minimal mass yet strong in compression or tension, and functional. But bees and spiders, unlike engineers, hadn't studied "theory of structures" at college, so what guiding hand had directed them? Come to that, if there really was some omnipotent force that shaped our destinies, why wasn't it doing something now about our predicament?

'Maybe it was sheer coincidence that just at this point in my musing we heard the sound of approaching aircraft. Twelve Typhoons were coming towards us. One of us fired a Very pistol and a few seconds later fired again. The leading Typhoon waggled his wings in acknowledgment. Eight of them continued to circle above us while the leader and three others flew back towards England. In a surprisingly short time they returned, escorting a Hudson with an airborne lifeboat slung underneath. This was dropped expertly within 30 yards of our dinghy and we were soon clambering aboard. Luxury at last! It was like moving up-market from a council house to a stately home. (There was that analogy again!)

'We soon had the lifeboat's engines going and headed for home. The rescue plane did likewise, escorted by four of the "Tiffies", while the remaining eight stayed overhead to protect us. This was more like it. How could I have entertained such unworthy doubts such a short while ago about the reliability of the good old guiding hand?

'But – hang on! If we had a master-planner looking after our interests, it was reasonable to believe that the enemy had one too, because at that moment a swarm of FW 190s were spotted heading our way. They were twice as many in number as our protective

Typhoons. Moreover, they had the advantage of height. The Typhoons climbed like mad to meet them and by the time they engaged the enemy they were some ten miles away from our lifeboat. In the battle that followed two FWs were shot down and the rest dispersed. One of them was downed by Squadron Leader Desmond Scott who, in turn, went into a spin while several thousand feet up, only recovering about 500 feet above the water and in time to see his victim's parachute billowing. An hour later the Germans attacked again. This time thirty FW 190s appeared, but Fighter Command had by then sent Spitfires to relieve the Typhoons. When the Nazis saw these roaring towards them they made no attempt to fight but turned tail for home. Meanwhile, two Air Sea Rescue high-speed launches had been sent out from England, one to take us aboard and the other to tow the lifeboat. Yet another up-market move, this time to home and safety. We landed at Newhaven, where the Royal Navy patched us up and whipped us off smartly to the Naval hospital at Swanborough, where we bathed, got into bed and were given a very welcome meal.

'More than 46 years later I was a guest of the Air Sea Rescue Service Association at one of their annual dinners. Their secretary, Jim Maton, had quietly arranged a surprise for me: he introduced me to the man who had pulled us aboard the rescue launch all those years ago. I can vaguely remember drinking his health once or twice that evening!'

The last word on this particular ditching is left to the Wellington's front gunner, Les W. Perkins, who vividly described the moment of impact in an article published by the American magazine *Airforce*.

'We were very low now, skimming just above the water, on and on, until with a sudden violent thump the tail made contact and thousands of gallons of water filled the aft sections. The crew was hit by a solid wall of water and I felt myself slammed hard against the main spar and turned sideways. The steel flare chute, torn loose from its moorings, struck me between the eyes and a million multi-coloured stars exploded in my head as I felt the cold green water dragging me under. I surfaced spluttering into the eerie silence. I was alone. Stunned and confused, I stared at the open astro hatch which seemed an impossible distance away. I attempted a step forward as the realization swept through me that I was not upright at all, but sitting at an angle tight against the bulkhead with my feet penetrating the fuselage. I was trapped. Panic! I pushed and pulled, jerking and twisting wildly. Nothing. I was firmly stuck.

'A dark bulk filled the hatch and a hand reached for mine, but our combined efforts were useless. I let go and stuck my head down under the water, feeling my way down my right leg to the crumpled geodetic section trapping my feet. With some difficulty I forced the zipper of my right boot open and resurfaced. I was soon free and standing on top of the fuselage with the skipper's arm around my waist. Weary and confused, I stared blankly around.

' "Where's the dinghy?" I mumbled. "Down there," replied Bray, pointing. Without hesitation I stepped into the sea.

'Helping hands grabbed me by my Mae West and the seat of my pants and deposited me unceremoniously into the dinghy. We were all safely aboard. We drifted slowly away from the sinking plane, watching its death with sadness. Quite suddenly, Wellington F for Freddie slid quietly beneath the water and disappeared.'

A YANK MEETS HIS SAVIOURS

In the Summer of 1994 at Lyme Regis a reunion of rescued airmen and their rescuers was organized by wartime veterans of the RAF Air Sea Rescue Service. One of those attending was James A. Myl, who had travelled all the way from California to offer thanks to his saviours.

An extract from his wartime personnel file reads as follows:-

'On 9 August, 1944, 1st Lt James A. Myl took off from Polebrook, England, on a bombing mission over Munich. Lt Myl was first pilot on a B-17 assigned to the 351st Bombardment Group, 511th Bombardment Squadron.

'The mission was recalled due to bad weather while Lt Myl's aircraft was over Holland. While flying over Belgium with five other B-17s, his aircraft was badly holed by flak, puncturing the right wing severely. It was not until the aircraft was over the North Sea, eighty miles from either coast, that the right wing caught fire in one immense sheet of flame.

'Noting at once that the fire was beyond control, Lt Myl gave the order to abandon ship and saw his crew take to their parachutes. Satisfied that his crew were safely out of the plane, Lt Myl then bailed out himself. His 'chute had not even opened when he heard the aircraft explode.

'Landing in the sea, Lt Myl heard his engineer, T/Sgt Lawrence Re, a non-swimmer, calling for assistance. Although the engineer was several hundred yards away, Lt Myl swam to him through the icy water. As a non-swimmer, depending entirely upon his Mae West lifejacket to keep him afloat, Sgt Re had failed to thrash his legs and arms about sufficiently, and, as a result, was suffering severely from the cold.

'Lt Myl told the Sergeant to keep his legs and arms moving constantly. He obtained benzedrine from the Sergeant's escape kit and gave it to him. While watching that the Sergeant's head did not slump into the water, he encouraged him with assurances that a P-51 Mustang, which had seen their aircraft go down in the North Sea, would soon send assistance when radio stations in England had completed fixing their position.

'After Lt Myl and Sgt Re had spent over three hours in the water, a British Air Sea Rescue launch operating out of Felixstowe found them and took them aboard.

'Aboard the launch, Lt Myl saw to it that the seven surviving members of his crew were given medical attention before accepting it himself. He also ascertained that the area had been thoroughly searched for the two missing crewmen before the launch headed for port.

'After returning to his base, Lt Myl and his fellow crewmen were de-briefed. Lt Myl was informed by the Awards and Decorations Officer of his squadron that he would be recommended for the Silver Star. Basis for the recommendation, the officer said, was that Lt Myl saved the lives of his crew by his cool judgment in giving the order to abandon ship immediately upon observing the outbreak of fire. The A. & D. Officer further stated that Lt Myl's action in swimming to the aid of Sergeant Re, thereby undoubtedly saving the Sergeant's life, constituted gallantry in itself deserving of the Silver Star.'

These were the words of an ancient official document, but Lt Myl has added his own comments. He was not awarded the Silver Star, and after 50 years the reasons can only be a matter of conjecture. Perhaps the necessary paperwork was never completed, or was lost. Perhaps it was recalled that he had been awarded a second DFC for a mission to Berlin only three days earlier, and the award of a Silver Star might be construed as 'piling it on'. Perhaps representation was forgotten in the feverish pace of flying combat missions in the early days of August, 1944. Perhaps it was because, not thinking or caring much about a decoration, he went home soon after. Finally, perhaps the explanation lies in a semi-official account of his crew's part in that mission to Munich, published in

The 351st Bomb Group in World War II, by Peter Harris and Ken Harbour:-

> 'August 9th 1944: Mission No.187. Lt Myl's plane was damaged over the target and forced to ditch in the channel. Before the crew could be picked up by Air Sea Rescue, Sgts McClure and Rasmussen had died of exposure.'

This, he says, is a mischaracterization of what actually occurred, and he has now given his own account of the events.

'I hadn't been at Polebrook long before I discovered that in the last 6½ months of 1943 the Group had flown 70 combat missions. From 15 June to 31 July, 1944, my own crew flew 24 combat missions – a total of 182 hours' flying. It was my impression that there were actually two air wars in Europe: the slower-paced war of the early days and, starting at about the time I arrived, the faster-paced war. In a way the latter played into our hands, because we wanted to complete our missions before the winter weather set in. I was offered additional training on an aircraft equipped to bomb accurately even through heavy cloud cover, but a consultation with my crew prompted me to decline. The consensus was: 'Let's finish as soon as possible and go home.' Well, we flew exactly as assigned, never aborted a single mission, and were later informed that we had completed one of the five fastest combat tours ever flown from England by the 8th Air Force.

'Another disturbing statistic involved probable losses. Send 1,500 four-engined bombers on a mission and the odds are that 50 aircraft, carrying 450–500 airmen, will be lost – that's a loss of one in 30 planes. And a full tour consisted of 35 missions. With odds like that in their favour, Las Vegas casinos could rake in some easy money.

'Weariness also became a plague. I set myself a strict regime: shower, eat, sleep and fly – no exceptions. I knew I was expendable, but never found the exact word to describe how I felt. Breathing pure oxygen helped. Somewhere early in my missions I began to breathe the delicious stuff from the ground up, rather than waiting till we'd climbed to the usual 10,000 feet to don the mask.

There was a penalty, however: the mask sawed back and forth across the ridge of my nose and opened a wound which never had time to heal.

'On 9 August, 1944, we flew our 29th mission. 1st Lt Anthony J. Zotollo led our 12-plane formation, while I flew closely behind him as leader of the low six-plane formation. The only members of my original ten-man crew (later reduced to nine) to fly with me that day were 2nd Lt Orville M. Bzoskie, co-pilot, T/Sgt Lawrence A. Re, engineer/top turret gunner, S/Sgt Merton H. Rasmussen, ball turret gunner and Leon D. Yurkus, waist gunner. Bzoskie was not only six years my senior but married, quiet, prayerful and reliable. Re (at 19, we called him 'the old man') was engaged: "One of these days in San Francisco we'll tie the knot," Larry would say, and he made good his promise. Moreover, when I married Dolores in 1948, Larry was my best man and his wife, Paula, a maid of honour.

'Flying with me for the first time that day were Michael O'Shea (navigator); my regular navigator had baled out over Berlin three days earlier and became a P.o.W. for the duration: Robert E. Pacquer, who flew as bombardier, T/Sgt Lester W. McClure (radioman) who replaced T/Sgt James B. Parten who had sustained injuries on our mission to Berlin so severe that he required lifelong medical treatment; Thomas V. Cardonna who was tail gunner.

'There was a sort of roulette of unattached crewmen on 511 Squadron. Many times, after telling me they knew a member of my regular crew, they would ask to be assigned to fly with me on the next mission. I took their names and numbers, but never asked any particular person to fly with me; nor did I discover why they asked random pilots to take them on combat missions.

'Somewhere over Holland our 12-aircraft formation entered thick cloud. Bzoskie shrugged as I flew on instruments while he kept lookout and made small corrections whenever he saw a plane ahead of us. This was a new and unwelcome experience: we had never flown blind before in close formation. "At least the fighters can't see us," I said. In retrospect, my attempt to stay loose must have left the crew thinking that fighters shooting at us might be preferable to flying blind in formation.

'A very small thing was probably the cause of our eventual

disaster. The lead plane's Pitot tube, the open end of which measures the windstream and translates it into airspeed, had frozen up. Zotollo as squadron leader relinquished the lead to Lawrence J. Dingle, his deputy: the daring manoeuvring to change positions in the leading three-plane element took on something of a dream-like quality. "Our early instructors in formation flying should see us now," I thought.

'A mission recall order was received and Dingle immediately led us into a gentle turn to starboard. Eventually we flew out of cloud cover, which had the appearance of a vertical wall, and into sparkling clear weather with stable air. Maybe such conditions prompted the scheduling of this mission. Because of our ability in formation flying (and a merciful God) the twelve aircraft stayed together through that terrible cloud cover.

'In straight and level flight towards the enemy coast at precisely 20,000 feet, we overflew a textbook flak attack near Antwerp in Belgium. Flak was nothing new, but this was the first time it was aimed to explode directly beneath our aircraft – unprecedented accuracy. The usual evasive action was not taken. It was as if Dingle was unaware of what was happening to the planes behind him and apparently no lookout told him of the attack. Zotollo's aircraft caught fire and peeled out of the formation; all the crew baled out near the island of Vlissingen, including navigator Wayne W. Livesay, who had flown with me only three days earlier to Berlin. He was captured and remained a P.o.W. for the duration.

'Over the North Sea, about eighty miles from either Antwerp or Felixstowe, flying at 8,500 feet, the right wing of our plane suddenly erupted in flame – a true internal wing fire. Un-controllable! Fire is a B-17's greatest nemesis. Think about it: slipping along at about 150 mph, the plane is loaded with mag-nesium, oxygen in tanks, 100-octane gasoline and rubber – not to mention bombs and bullets. I had already seen several B-17s ignite and explode in midair. I made a quick decision, seconded by Bzoskie, to order the crew to bale out. By my count the crew, some wearing back-pack parachutes and others with buckle-on-chest type, were clear of the plane in seven seconds.

'I pulled my ripcord and felt a horrendous jerk when the 'chute opened. I was floating under a huge nylon canopy towards the seemingly endless sea. I counted eight parachutes below: everyone was out. As a lifeguard on Long Beach before entering the Army Air Corps, I had often used canvas airbags to float and ride on the waves, and I thought I would try to recover my 'chute. Its size and whiteness would be an ideal marker and maybe it would be useful as an airbag type raft.

'These thoughts were going through my mind when out of the blue came a guardian angel: a lone P-51 Mustang pilot flew his sleek aircraft past me at about 200 yards distance. I saluted, never more pleased to see another human being.

'With back to the wind, I splashed down into the North Sea. When I had sunk to the limit I lunged up backwards. My parachute was in front of me, like an arrow, dragging me under again and harder to handle than I had thought. The time on my watch – still running – showed that there would be plenty of daylight remaining. I had to settle for cutting out roughly two panels of my 'chute and allowing the rest to sink. That, and an escape kit which blew out of my flying suit's pocket, were the only items of equipment that I lost.

'There was still the (and never more beautiful) sound of the Mustang circling above us. My prayer was that he could make contact on the emergency radio channel so that our position could be fixed by triangulation. (I was later to learn that this pilot, flying with the 355th Fighter Group from Steeple Morden, landed on the first runway he could find in England and ran out of fuel as he landed.)

'I then heard Larry Re, a non-swimmer, calling from somewhere out of sight. Calling on unexpected reserves of energy, I swam for about ninety minutes before I reached him. He was really cold and blue-faced. I told him to thrash about with arms and legs. By contrast, I felt almost sweaty, but that was short-lived. At that point I inflated my Mae West lifejacket but it was woefully inadequate, providing too much buoyancy for the stomach and almost none for the head, so that anyone unconscious or unable to tread water fairly vigorously would surely drown when his head dipped below the water.

'Soon I was overtaken by brutal cold; my teeth chattered uncontrollably. I felt a small filling, or part of a broken tooth, in my mouth; I could neither spit it out nor pick it out and bit my finger trying to prise it out. As a last desperate resort, I swallowed it; I subsequently determined it had been a filling.

'The salt water played hell with the open wound across the bridge of my nose caused by the friction of my oxygen mask. The only comfort was the Mustang circling overhead. Larry and I tried to fill the time by singing and slapping each other's arms. The nagging question was, had our lone friend been able to summon help?

' "I wish I had a cigarette," Larry said. That set me thinking about my dad. Twice gassed in World War I in France, he had continued to smoke heavily until he died at the age of 64. His example led me to pledge that I would never smoke. Wrong! Returning from my first combat mission, Larry had offered me a cigarette and, stupidly, I took it. Then I was hooked and continued to smoke from June, 1944 until I finally quit in 1977. But Larry's statement called for a reply. "I wish we could both have a smoke," I said.

'At last, overhead came the drone of two P-47 Thunderbolts, which dropped flares, water markers and an inflatable raft or two. Just in time! Larry and I were almost "goners". We searched the horizon for a launch, and there it was, working its way upwind, taking aboard survivors. Larry and I were the last to be picked up. The launch's rope ladder was like a stairway to Heaven. As I began to climb I found I could not lower my arms. Two British sailors helped me aboard and used some force to lower my arms. From that time on, I've paid the price of their well-intentioned effort with frequent muscle haemorrhages.

'I told the skipper there were nine of us, but only seven of us were aboard. A quick head count revealed that S/Sgt Rasmussen and T/Sgt McClure were still missing. The launch made a wide sweep of the area without sighting them. Navigator Michael O'Shea later reminded me that the two missing men were the only members of the crew equipped with one-man dinghies. My own speculation was that the two men faced the wind as they struck the water, and surfaced to find themselves covered over and enmeshed in their parachutes. Even if the Mae Wests had been inflated, they could possibly have died of suffocation.

'Our saviours stripped our wet clothing and gave us blankets and heavy woollen, hip-length stockings. In the water my watch had never missed a beat, but two days later its plastic was waffled and the innards were a total wreck.

'The RAF Air Sea Rescue launch, which the British called "a nice little boat", beat its way for several hours to dock at Felixstowe, where we survivors were hospitalized overnight. As we warmed up, the chatter about our miraculous escape escalated. Next day one of our Squadron's aircraft flew us back to base. I wrote letters to the next of kin of the two missing crew members, but never received a single word in reply.

'Our crew was sent on ten days' leave at a so-called "Flak House" at Southport. Several evenings we were entertained on a grand piano by an airman who was second to none as a jazz pianist, with another flyer on double bass; amazing that they were not assigned to Special Services as musicians. We were also interviewed about our North Sea episode by two inspectors, and I believe that as a result the existing Mae Wests were removed from service and replaced by new life preservers providing far more buoyancy behind the neck.

'After hitching a ride on a B-17 to Bassingbourn, I caught the train from Cambridge to London and checked into the Piccadilly Hotel. Never before had I experienced anything like Piccadilly Circus at night. Blackout conditions were in force, of course, but troops of many nationalities were shoulder to shoulder on the pavement. Every tenth person appeared to be a "pimp" – taxis were being used as mobile brothels rather than transport. One day I was taking a nap when London suffered a daylight "buzz-bomb" attack. Outside my door the hall was wall-to-wall with people running in opposite directions – Americans to the roof for a better view, British to the bomb shelters for better seats. I stood in the doorway to the roof when the buzz-bomb engine suddenly died. I saw it continue on course for a short distance and then plunge downwards. It seemed to be falling directly towards me, but no – it struck the roof of the Air Ministry building. There was a tremendous explosion, lots of smoke and the noise of breaking glass. Windows on the block were shattered, but no one was killed.

'After returning to Peterborough by train and reporting to my squadron, on the tenth day of my leave I flew an eight-and-a-half hour combat mission to Weimar. Near to the end of August I counted down towards my final days of flying combat missions from Polebrook. I knew in my heart that I was no longer as good a pilot as I had been three weeks earlier. The weight of those recent events depressed me. Lester McClure and Merton Rasmussen were both "missing in action" and their names recorded on the Memorial Wall at Cambridge. James Parten, while flying with me on the mission to Berlin, had a German fighter's 20 mm shell explode in his lap and his grievous injuries required lifetime treatment. Ellis Tomkins, my regular navigator, stayed in Germany as a P.o.W. for the duration. Fifty years later, I remember those few mean weeks of the English summer of 1944 with great sadness.'

...AND THE ENGINES FELL OUT

In the small hours of 15 September, 1940, a Whitley bomber of 10 Squadron was returning to base after a raid on Antwerp. One engine had been damaged during the raid and eventually gave up the ghost when the aircraft was about 20 miles short of the coast at Spurn Head. The pilot, Squadron Leader F. Ferguson, carried out a very satisfactory ditching and the dinghy was launched successfully.

There was only one minor casualty. In his haste to leave the rear turret, air gunner Mark Niman went head first into the large metal tail-wheel spar which he was supposed to climb across in order to reach the rear hatch. A few hours later he had a massive egg-shaped lump on his forehead.

After bouncing around in the dinghy for a few hours, the crew were sighted by a Royal Navy minesweeper, HMS *Kurd*. This was a 200-ton vessel which had just laid a minefield in the area in which they had ditched.

The crew of the Whitley were told later that there had been some reluctance aboard HMS *Kurd* to pick up the airmen until it had been firmly established that they were British. One of the sailors said in no uncertain terms that if it had been otherwise, their flying boots would have been removed and they would have been returned to the 'oggin'.

In the event, however, the rescuers proved to be wonderful and caring hosts, though this was not fully appreciated by the Whitley crew at the time, who were kept aboard HMS *Kurd* for the next two days while minesweeping and minelaying activities continued. However, on eventually being landed at Grimsby, they were taken on a pub-crawl by the Navy and any lack of understanding between the two Services was quickly dissipated.

*   *   *

Less than a year later, on 5 July, 1941, Sgt Mark Niman took off from Redruth in Cornwall in a Bombay aircraft, which was to be delivered to 216 Squadron at Heliopolis, near Cairo. The journey was to be made in three legs: Redruth-Gibraltar, Gibraltar-Malta and finally Malta-Cairo. The aircraft had been fitted with special inboard ballast tanks to carry the extra fuel required. Sgt Niman had never been abroad before and was looking forward to the trip with some excitement.

As the aircraft headed for Gibraltar Sgt Niman twiddled the knobs on his R.1082 radio to obtain DF bearings on his loop aerial which were passed back to the navigator. At daybreak the second pilot passed by the radio cabin on his way to the ballast tanks, where he was required to pump fuel from this reserve into the wing tanks. Shortly afterwards, Sgt Niman looked out of his window to see a stream of petrol flowing off the trailing edge of the wing. He reported this immediately to the pilot, who ordered the second pilot to return to the controls. There followed a rather unnerving conversation on the intercom, when the two pilots agreed that there was probably not enough fuel left for the Bombay to reach Gibraltar.

Sgt Niman wasted no time in getting an approximate position from the navigator, changing his transmitter to the distress frequency and sending out an SOS.

Sure enough, about fifteen minutes later the engines cut. Sgt Niman says the pilot made an excellent ditching, 'Not much worse then his normal landings'. He felt it was even more remarkable in view of the fact that the Bombay was a fixed-undercarriage aircraft.

The dinghy was prepared, but the Bombay appeared to be floating quite comfortably, probably because of the now empty ballast tanks, although the fuselage was half full of water. The crew climbed up on to the wings, taking the Very distress pistol, and began to sunbathe while they waited for someone to arrive. Fortunately, they learned subsequently that the SOS had been picked up. Two hours after the ditching, an RAF Air Sea Rescue launch, ML 161 from Gibraltar, reached the stricken Bombay.

First they took the crew aboard and then the saturated bags of mail. They decided that, as the aircraft was still afloat, they would try to tow it back to Gibraltar, some ten miles distant. Two large hawsers were soon fastened to the engines of the Bombay and the launch moved gently forward.

Yes, the *launch* moved forward. All that happened to the Bombay was that the two great engines fell out into the water. Mark Niman says there was not the slightest shudder from the aircraft. The engines appeared simply to fall off, as though they had been kept in place by chewing gum.

The Bombay crew enjoyed a brief holiday on the Rock and at La Linea before returning to England by ship, to collect and fly another Bombay to Heliopolis. This, fortunately, was accomplished without incident.

ALL IN VAIN

There can hardly be a more tragic story, nor one which so vividly epitomizes the bravery of the crews of RAF Air Sea Rescue launches, than the record of High Speed Launch (HSL) 138. Built by the British Power Boat Company at Hythe, Southampton, in 1941/2, this launch was 63 feet long and was powered by three 500 hp Napier 'Sea Lion' engines, giving it a speed of 16 knots. The defensive armament consisted normally of a single .303 Vickers or Lewis gun in each enclosed turret (later twin Vickers guns were mounted on either side of the wheelhouse) and a 20 mm Oerlikon cannon or 0.5 mm Browning.

Based originally at Calshot, HSL 138 was operating from No.27 Air Sea Rescue Unit at Dover when it was sent into action on 15 July, 1942. A Spitfire piloted by the well-known Battle of Britain personality, Wing Commander 'Paddy' Finucane, DSO, DFC, had been shot down over the Channel, about 7 miles south-west of Boulogne, by German fighters. Two HSLs and 2 MLs were ordered to attempt a rescue. The launches had made a rendezvous in the Channel that morning to back up an RAF fighter sweep off the French coast and had later taken up separate stations.

Up to that time an unwritten code of conduct had been observed both by the RAF and the Luftwaffe in effecting rescues of 'ditched' airmen. It was understood that if we did not interfere or shoot up German rescue craft, they would reciprocate. In July, 1942, the peace was shattered.

HSL 138 was east of Dover and its companion vessel, HSL 140, stood off to the west. After being on station for some time they were instructed to carry out 'square searches' near Le Touquet. Crewman A. Scarratt, a Nursing Orderly, was in the front gun turret of HSL 140, keeping an eye open for any sign of a dinghy and at the same time glancing skywards for enemy aircraft. At about 1.15 p.m. he spotted three layers of FW 190s circling Le Touquet. Shortly afterwards he was appalled to find that their boat was being attacked from astern. The unwritten law was being broken. The rear gunner returned fire and there were claims that a FW 190 had been shot down. Down below, the radio operator was calling for assistance from Dover and giving the vessel's position.

The German fighters carried out only one attack at that stage and then disappeared, presumably returning to a French base to refuel. HSL 140 had not been damaged during the attack and there were no injuries. HSL 138 then approached in company with one of the motor launches; after a short exchange between the skippers, a radio instruction was received to proceed to the east and carry out further square searches. HSL 138 and the motor launch were left on station near Le Touquet.

Nursing Orderly Scarratt continues the story:-

'We had not been under way for more than a minute when the 190s returned to the attack, raking the whole length of the boat from astern. The gunner who had earlier claimed to have shot down a 190 was killed and several other crew members were injured. The skipper and I came up on deck to see what was happening. I saw hordes of 190s attacking our launch from astern and from both sides. I also saw that HSL 138 and the motor launch were also under attack. One of the enemy aircraft dropped a bomb on HSL 138, sinking it immediately. My opposite number on 138, Bill Morgan, was killed and went down with the launch, but not before he had carried out his duties attending to casualties sustained during the attack. Survivors of 138 told me later that Bill received wounds to the ankles and had his forearm blown off, but still continued to care for the wounded. He was last seen lying below decks, having been hit in the chest by a cannon shell. Only minutes before this happened I had spoken to Bill, who had been best man at my wedding two weeks earlier. I had the unenviable task of sorting out his possessions. They included a small silver shoe from my wedding cake which he had kept in the top pocket of his tunic. He was a gallant airman.'

HSL 140 was still under continuous attack; the skipper took command of the launch from the port side of the deck and told the coxswain to take evasive action as the vessel was being attacked from both sides. The gunners were firing at will from the stern, using the twin Vickers machine guns. Several other crew members were injured and in view of the impossible odds the skipper, F. O. Shaker, decided to return to base. HSL 140 headed flat out for Dover, taking evasive action all the way; the attacks by the FW 190s, which had continued for about twenty minutes, only ceased as the vessel drew near to the English coast. Nursing Orderly Scarratt commented, 'If it had not been for the presence of mind of our skipper in taking command from the deck we would also have been sunk with HSL 138. He certainly saved our lives that day.'

When the vessel finally docked at Dover, badly shot up and with the crew in a state of shock, they were met by the Commanding Officer, Squadron Leader Coates, and several ambulances with naval officers in attendance. As Nursing Orderly Scarratt was leaving the launch he was asked to return with a naval medical officer to examine the gunner who had been killed. 'He was not a pleasant sight,' he says.

He also pays tribute to the motor launch which came to 140's assistance. 'I must say I have always had the greatest admiration for the skipper and crew of this vessel. During the initial attack on HSL 138, the motor launch stood stock still and fought off the attacks; at the same time, crew members were picking up survivors of the HSL.'

The day after the action the uninjured survivors were given three days' leave. On return to duty, Nursing Orderly Scarratt went to see HSL 140 in the repair slips at Snargate Street dock. He was amazed at the extent of the damage: the petrol tanks were peppered with holes like a colander, the rear turret was smashed in and the deck riddled with bullet and cannon shell holes.

The escorting Canadian Spitfires from 402 Squadron flew back to Le Touquet the following day and dropped a wreath on the sea where HSL 138 had gone down.

Several awards were subsequently made to members of the crew of HSL 138 who survived, including Distinguished Service Medals to Corporal O'Sullivan and A.C.1. Whitlock. While recovering from the wounds he had received, the skipper of 138, Flying Officer Walters, was tragically killed in the Café de Paris, London, destroyed in a German night bombing attack.

Nor did the motor launch crews return unscathed: on ML 141 an officer was killed and three ratings wounded, while two officers and two ratings were wounded on ML 139.

The search for Paddy Finucane was all in vain. He did not survive.

SUCH LANGUAGE!

All too often these stories of ditched airmen carry an element of tragedy. Occasionally, however, a flash of humour breaks through.

In August, 1940, John Gibson was an acting Flight Lieutenant flying Hurricanes in the Battle of Britain with 501 Squadron from Hawkinge in Kent. On the evening of the 29th the Squadron was scrambled to intercept Messerschmitt 109s at 15,000 feet over the Channel. In the ensuing dog-fight John Gibson's Hurricane was damaged by enemy fire and he was forced to bale out. He spent nearly an hour in the water before being rescued by a high-speed launch and taken to Dover. His own account of the incident is worth reproducing:

'I was picked up in the Channel by the Royal Navy, who, after sighting me, raced to my position in a good old "gung-ho" fashion at about 30 knots. At the last moment, when almost upon me, the launch did a split-arse 180 degree turn, went into full reverse and nosed up to me, pointing a Lewis gun and shouting the ridiculous "friend or foe?" challenge. Since they had almost drowned me in their wash (I was only wearing the old type Mae West), my reply was hardly friendly, but left the sailor with the gun in no doubt that I was *not* one of the enemy.

'I was told later that on a previous rescue they had encountered some overly brave Luftwaffe idiot who had waved his Luger pistol at them.

'Getting aboard the Vosper was a bit tricky, as this launch was not normally used for air-sea rescue and carried no rope ladder. However, with the use of a rope with a noose which I was told to put round one of my feet, and the help of two or three brawny sailors on the other end, I made the five or six feet to the deck in a manner in which I have seen tunny and tuna fish hauled out of the sea.

'Once aboard, I was looked after very well, given dry clothes in the shape of bell-bottom trousers and a roll-neck sweater, a tin mug and some Scotch (but no water). By the time I reached Dover I was pretty happy. I was met by a Lieutenant-Commander surgeon who took me to an hotel commandeered by the Navy, where he prescribed more whisky.

'I was driven back to Gravesend in a large car with two WRENS, where I was met by our Squadron Commander, Harry Hogan. In his generosity the great man told me to get some sleep, as I had to be on readiness again at four o'clock next morning.'

John Gibson went on to win the DSO and the DFC, serving for a while in the Pacific with a New Zealand squadron before returning to Europe in 1944 to join a Tempest squadron in Holland.

SINK THAT LANCASTER

Berlin. No doubt more than a few hearts began to flutter among bomber crews when the 'target for tonight' was announced as Germany's capital city. It was a long trip, across the heart of enemy territory, with flak and night fighters in abundance.

On 29 December, 1943, a Mark II Lancaster of 514 Squadron based at Waterbeach took off for the big target. Before reaching Berlin they were attacked by a JU 88. After an exchange of fire, what appeared to be a rocket projectile exploded just beneath the Lancaster's port wing. The JU 88 disappeared and they flew on.

By 10 p.m. the Lancaster had dropped its bombs and was heading for home. At almost the same location as before, they were again attacked by a JU 88. This time the gunners were convinced that they had successfully hit the enemy aircraft when they saw it wobble, as if out of control, and a red glow appeared in the centre of the fuselage. They would claim it as a 'probable'.

Fifteen minutes later they were involved in yet another 'punch-up' with a JU 88, but there was no apparent damage and no casualties. But it had been noticed that the Lancaster was seriously short of petrol, possibly caused by damage to the port wing during the first enemy fighter attack.

The bomber continued on course for Waterbeach, but base proved to be a few gallons too far. Soon after 10 p.m. the captain ordered 'ditching stations' and brought the Lancaster down on to the North Sea.

There had been some controversy over the ditching qualities of the Mark II Lancaster. The popular conception was that the large frontal area of the radial engines would not permit so smooth an entry to the water as the streamlined form of the cowled Merlins, but statistics showed that the Hercules-powered Halifax bombers

46

had a better record for safe ditching than the Merlin-engined Lancaster.

The incident on the night of 29/30 December proved the point to the Squadron's satisfaction. Sgt Leslie Weddle from Northumberland, the Flight Engineer, takes up the story:-

'After ditching at about 10 p.m., we scrambled out on to the aircraft's wings. We had to chop the dinghy out of the wing, as it had not self-inflated. It was very cold and the sea was very rough. We huddled together for warmth. We were about 70 miles from the English coast.

'At daybreak next morning we spotted a Lancaster and sent up a Very light which guided it to our position. Needless to say, we were overjoyed when they flashed a message to say that we should hang on – help was on the way. Shortly after that a Liberator dropped us another dinghy – just as well, since ours was leaking.

'At about 2 p.m. on 30 December we were finally picked up by a high-speed launch of the Air Sea Rescue Service and taken to Yarmouth. We had a medical examination before flying back to Waterbeach.'

This Lancaster crew were lucky. Not only did they survive the three enemy fighter attacks and the subsequent ditching without loss or injury, but they had a Flight Commander who set a splendid example of how to fulfil a commanding officer's responsibility. Even though he knew that Air Sea Rescue services had been alerted, Wing Commander Sansom did not leave it at that. Before dawn he had raised a scratch crew and taken off in a Lancaster on a planned search pattern. On his very first leg a Very light was spotted. As they headed towards it, a dinghy became visible with several men aboard. For no less then three hours Wing Commander Sansom circled the dinghy, calling up rescue craft. Eventually other aircraft arrived and a rescue launch arrived on the scene. All seven crew members were safely transferred. Wing Commander Sansom himself flew the crew back to Waterbeach.

The postscript to this story concerns the doubts that had been voiced concerning the buoyancy of the Mark II Lancaster. Twelve hours after the ditching, the aircraft was still afloat and eventually had to be sunk. There was general satisfaction on 514 Squadron: this was their first Lancaster ditching.

Crew of Lancaster:
F.O. L. Greenburgh (pilot); Sgt P. Butler (navigator); Sgt D. Bament (bomb aimer); Sgt G. Stromberg (W.op/AG); Sgt L. Weddle (flight engineer); Sgt F. Carey (mid-upper gunner); F/Sgt C. Drake (rear gunner)

IN A RUBBER RING

In the Autumn of 1944 Flight Sergeant Donald M. Kennedy was flying on Beaufighters as navigator/wireless operator with 489 Squadron of the Royal New Zealand Air Force, based at Langham in Norfolk.

On the night of 3 October F/Sgt Kennedy took off with his New Zealand pilot, Warrant Officer D. H. Mann, with orders to attack a German convoy off the Dutch coast. The aircraft carried torpedos.

As they began their attack at about a hundred feet above the sea, the Beaufighter hit something which badly damaged the starboard wing. The aircraft's speed dropped from 200 knots to well under 100 – perilously close to the Beaufighter's stalling speed. The outcome was a belly flop into the North Sea close to Terschelling.

These two luckless airmen spent almost eight days in their dinghy before being rescued by HSL 2679, commanded by Flying Officer Ross and based at Gorleston near Great Yarmouth. F/Sgt Kennedy comments, 'October is not a very nice month in the North Sea and I spent most of it sitting in the rubber ring called a dinghy.'

FLIGHT ENGINEER/ORGANIST

The bed of the North Sea will be strewn with the remains of Second World War aircraft of every shape and size. One of them will be a Stirling of 15 Squadron.

Herbert Brodie's background, before he joined the RAF, was interesting. He had managed his father's grocery and provisions business at Willington Quay in Northumberland and he was an accomplished organist; he had played the cinema organ at the Princes Theatre, North Shields, and was assistant organist at St John's Methodist Church at Whitley Bay. 'And now for something completely different,' as the comedian might remark. Herbert Brodie went into the RAF and qualified as Flight Engineer, joining 15 Squadron at Mildenhall to fly Stirlings.

On the night of 24 June, 1943, the target was Wuppertal. All was quiet until the aircraft, piloted by F/Sgt Towse from Cardiff, crossed the Dutch coast. A JU88 approached the bomber, but apparently without seeing it; it closed in until the pilot could distinguish the black crosses on the fuselage. It then broke away in a climb, and at this point the front gunner opened fire, raking the JU88 from stem to stern. It turned over on one wingtip and plunged vertically out of sight.

The Stirling continued on course to Wuppertal and bombed the target. Soon afterwards, however, it was hit by flak; the fuel tanks were holed, and the petrol ignited. The rear gunner, Sgt J. A. Baldwin of Immingham, saw the flames streaming from the wing and almost simultaneously, Warrant Officer Brodie called out the warning, 'Starboard wing on fire!'

The pilot ordered the crew to prepare to bale out. He put the Stirling into a steep dive and successfully extinguished the fire, but a large hole had been burnt in the wing. The aircraft flew on over the North Sea, but fuel was very low, and the pilot finally ditched about 20 miles east of Felixstowe in the early hours of 25 June.

As the Stirling hit the water it broke into two halves and sank in about ten seconds. The navigator, Sgt J. Barass of Hull, was washed up through the astrodome and hauled aboard the dinghy. The pilot was obliged to tear his harness free before he could climb out of the front escape hatch and he succeeded in the nick of time as the Stirling began to sink.

Fortunately the crew spent little more than two hours in the dinghy before they were picked up by Air Sea Rescue HSL 121 based at Felixstowe, escorted by a pair of Typhoons. The wireless operator, Norman J. Pawley, was awarded the DFM after this flight.

For Herbert Brodie, all this excitement was not the climax of his RAF career. Less than two months later his aircraft was shot down over Germany and he spent the rest of the war in a prison camp.

FROM MONTREAL INTO THE MED.

In 1940 Bob Middlemiss, living in Montreal, was preparing to attend the University of California. By that time, however, the plight of the 'Mother Country' at war was broadcast daily and Bob was aware of the desperate need for help. His father, an immigrant from London, had fought in the First World War and had again enlisted. So his son followed the family tradition and enlisted in the Royal Canadian Air Force in September.

After his initial training in Ontario he left for the U.K. At Hawarden he had 35 hours' training in Spitfires prior to joining 145 Squadron at Catterick. His stay there was short and he was soon posted to 41 Squadron, part of the Tangmere wing.

In February, 1942, he was on escort duty to bombers attacking the German battleships *Scharnhorst*, *Gneisenau*, and *Prinz Eugen* and a few weeks later, on a sweep over France, he claimed his first 'kill' – an FW 190.

Then came a posting to 249 Squadron, based in Malta. Part of the journey from Britain was made on the aircraft carrier HMS *Eagle*. The fighters took off amid heavy fire from escort ships which were warding off an enemy attack by JU 88s. Before the fighters could land at Malta they were engaged by ME 109s; four aircraft and their pilots were lost. With very little fuel to spare, the survivors limped into Takali airfield on the island.

During June Bob successfully shot down three enemy aircraft: a Macchi 202, an ME 109 and a Cant Z1007 (a three-engined Italian bomber).

On 7 July he sat in readiness with nine other pilots when an order came through to scramble eight fighters, leaving Bob Middlemiss and Raoul Daddo-Langlois grounded. At that time, on the George Cross island, everyone agreed that it was safer in the air than on the ground. So Bob and 'Daddo' persuaded the controller to let them join their airborne colleagues. Having lost time in the delay, they climbed swiftly to gain height. Suddenly they saw the German bombers, JU 88s, at the same height, and although realizing that enemy fighters must be waiting at a higher level they decided to attack the bombers.

Daddo-Langlois turned in and got one of the JU 88s, but Bob noticed that an ME 109 was preparing to attack. He went at the 109 and saw strikes along the length of the aircraft. Knowing that Daddo could not be far away, he turned and looked over his left shoulder. Bob Middlemiss himself continues the story:

'Suddenly my right hand left the stick with the impact of being shot in the right arm and back. Had I not been sitting back and looking over my left shoulder, I would have been a goner. The Spitfire was in a spin and smoking. I was unable to eject because of the centrifugal force, but I managed to roll the aircraft over and fall out. I opened the parachute and drifted down, eventually landing in the water. I shed the parachute and pulled out my dinghy. The words went through my mind: "Slowly turn the tap of the CO_2 bottle". To my dismay, as I frantically continued turning, I discovered that the bottle was empty. With my right arm useless, I had problems trying to attach the bellows pump to the dinghy; the cord attached to the dinghy kept getting in the way, but I finally took out my knife and cut the cord, held the dinghy with my bad arm while I screwed in the pump and began the inflation. After a while there was enough air in the dinghy to allow me to climb in and begin paddling towards the island.

'I had been shot down on the eastern side of Malta, but unfortunately the Squadron were searching for me on the western side. Only when Paul Brennan (RAAF) and Sergeant de l'Ara flew out on patrol to protect some minesweepers was I spotted in the drink. They made one pass over me and then approached again. I thought of jumping into the sea in case they attacked the dinghy. However, they waggled their wings and I breathed again. Shortly afterwards, High Speed Launch 128 reached me: I was hauled aboard, wrapped in blankets and given a shot of Navy rum – which nearly made my eyes pop out.

'Later I saw the holes in my arm. The surgeon who operated on my back said I had missed death by about a quarter of an inch.'

As a result of his injuries, Bob returned to England. After a spell as instructor at an Operational Training Unit he was posted to 403 Squadron at Kenley under the famous Johnnie Johnson. After three tours of operations he was transferred back to Canada. Soon after, on his wedding day, he heard he had been awarded the DFC, a wonderful wedding present.

When the war ended Bob remained in the RCAF and was eventually given command of the first Squadron (427) of the New Starfighters, based at Zweibrücken in Germany, with the rank of Wing Commander.

His story ends on a tragic note. A year later he flew back to Germany from London with his family on a Bristol Freighter: the plane crashed, killing all on board, including his wife, with the exception of one airman, Bob himself and his daughter.

WHERE SHALL WE GO NEXT?

To fly a Lancaster to Berlin in the latter years of the war was certainly no picnic; but how much more hazardous the mission must have been in December, 1940, in a Whitley bomber, notoriously slow and carrying none of the electronic navigational aids which later became standard equipment.

At that time Whitleys were being flown by 102 (Ceylon) Squadron, operating from Linton-on-Ouse after having been bombed out of their home base at Driffield by JU 88s in August, 1940.

One of the pilots was Sergeant Harold ('Jim') Chapman. On the night of 15 December they took off for Berlin. The co-pilot was Squadron Leader Morris, acting CO at Linton-on-Ouse, who flew about every tenth trip with a different crew to maintain morale. For the wireless operator, it was his first operational sortie.

After bombing the target, the Whitley was badly damaged by flak; both the wireless transmitter and air-to-ground radio (R/T) were put out of action and the return journey had to be made on dead reckoning navigation, hopefully with the aid of some fixes obtained by the wireless operator with his receiver and loop aerial, which was undamaged. However, none was forthcoming. It was felt that the strain of the mission had proved too much for the unblooded wireless operator, who was later reported to be taken off flying duties.

The dead reckoning navigation brought the Whitley satisfactorily back to the English coast at Bridlington. On reaching Linton-on-Ouse, however, the airfield was found to be covered in dense fog. With complete lack of communication facilities with the ground, it was impossible to make a safe landing through the blanket of fog.

The Squadron Leader suggested that the Whitley be flown back to the coast in order to follow the railway line from Bridlington to Driffield, where the fog might be less dense and a landing attempted. Jim Chapman put the CO's suggestion to the test, but repeatedly lost sight of the railway lines in the fog. This plan had to be abandoned, and the Whitley headed south in the hope of making an emergency landing before the fuel, which was very low, was completely exhausted.

Sure enough the fog finally disappeared, but every suitable landing site was seen to have been dug with ditches or dotted with poles. This was the time when the threat of a German invasion was very real indeed.

By this time both pilots were very weary, having been in the air for eleven hours or more. Jim Chapman was taking a welcome rest when he suddenly remembered one of his training lectures during which it had been suggested that, if a certain signal were given to a searchlight battery, they would lay their beams flat and point to a safe area for an emergency landing.

The navigator, Pilot Officer Operon, eagerly looked up the appropriate signal in his manual and the Whitley circled a search-light battery, flashing the signal on the aircraft's lower identification light. For what seemed an eternity there was no response. Then, quite suddenly, all the beams were laid in one direction and the Whitley turned on to the line in which they were pointing.

The crew's euphoria was short-lived. The beams led them straight back over the North Sea. Maybe the ack-ack boys were taking no chances in case the aircraft was an enemy intruder; maybe they had had a previous 'dust-up' with the RAF. Whatever the reason, the Whitley crew were not best pleased and began once more to search for a suitable landing ground.

Jim Chapman was now back at the controls and decided to try for a landing on Flamborough Head, where there seemed to be no obstructions. The Whitley's wheels had actually touched the ground when out of the fog, directly ahead, loomed a building. Jim pulled back desperately on the control column and felt the wheels touch the roof of the building. Beyond it there was nothing; they had flown over the edge of a cliff.

The Whitley continued its climb to about a thousand feet. At this point Jim turned the aircraft to head back towards the land. Then, without warning, both engines spluttered and died. The fuel tanks were empty. Jim shouted, 'Ditching!' but there was no time for the crew to take up the proper positions before the Whitley hit the waves.

The bottom escape hatch burst open and a jet of water hit Jim in the chest. The wireless operator and navigator managed to open the rear door, which by this time was also under water. Squadron Leader Morris climbed through the top hatch and Jim handed him the Very pistol and cartridges.

The Whitley was settling quickly in the water; in theory its maximum flotation time was five minutes. The CO, navigator and wireless operator were now on top of the fuselage above the rear door, but there was no sign of the rear gunner. At long last a hatch in front of the turret opened and he emerged.

It was decided that it was too risky to re-enter the aircraft to retrieve the dinghy, fastened inside the rear door. Instead, the crew would remain on top of the fuselage for as long as possible. Jim Chapman recalls that in his panic he pulled the pin to inflate his Mae West, which blew up so rapidly that it almost broke his neck.

The crew stood at the centre of the fuselage, hanging on to the wireless aerial. It was very cold indeed. Jim reluctantly kicked off his 'lovely black flying boots', which he had had since 1938, in case he had to swim. The Whitley was sinking slowly below the water line and eventually the crew were up to their chests in water.

Far in the distance there were faint lights, presumably Bridlington. The Squadron Leader fired off a Very cartridge at roughly half-hour intervals and finally they were rewarded by the sound of a boat's engine. Fortunately the aircraft had sunk no further.

As the crew waited anxiously for the boat, the engine suddenly died and all was quiet. Another half-hour passed and the last Very cartridge was fired. Then came the sound of oars, and into sight appeared an off-shore fisherman's boat. It had run out of petrol.

Two men rowed the boat over the submerged wing of the Whitley and the crew were taken aboard. Just before the navigator left the aircraft, the aerial snapped and rapped itself round him. He almost drowned before his colleagues could disentangle him from the wire.

The crew were landed at Bridlington harbour and taken into a small stone building, possibly a coastguard post, and given pint mugs of steaming tea. Jim says he has never tasted tea like it, before or since. A van collected the crew and returned them to Linton-on-Ouse. They had been in the air for almost twelve hours.

Jim Chapman records that in addition to losing his precious flying boots, he had also lost his cap. On the afternoon following the ditching he awoke very hungry. There were no mess facilities in his billet at Benningborough Hall, and he decided to walk to the nearby village for 'tea and a wad'. On the way back he was picked up by an RAF bus and sat in the only vacant seat next to the Station Adjutant. On reporting for duty the next morning, he found himself 'on a charge' for not wearing proper uniform and received a severe reprimand. He was not too impressed.

Walking with an RAF friend along Bridlington promenade on Christmas morning, Jim was flabbergasted to see his Whitley bomber on the beach, with airmen working on it. It seems that the empty fuel tanks and balloon tyres had kept the aircraft afloat below the surface of the water until it was washed ashore by the tide nine days later.

DON'T GO OUT THAT WAY

The war in Europe was almost over when Sgt William Fleming was stationed at Great Dunmow, Essex, flying Horsa Mark 1 gliders. At nearby Matching Green airfield he and his fellow glider pilots had the unnerving experience of being towed in practice flights by 'tug' crews who were still under training. In March, 1945, however, practice ended and, after Sgt Fleming and the rest of his flight had been confined to barracks, briefing began for 'Operation Varsity' – the crossing of the Rhine.

During the build-up to the operation Sgt Fleming received a letter from his mother. He and his whole family were devout Christians and his mother had sent him an extract from Deuteronomy, chapter 33 verse 27: 'The eternal God is thy refuge and underneath are the everlasting arms.' Sgt Fleming accepted this as God's promise to him for the great day ahead.

On 24 March his glider was loaded with a jeep and trailer carrying mortars and ammunition, and a motor cycle; also aboard were an officer, a corporal and five other ranks from the Oxfordshire & Buckinghamshire Regiment.

Take-off was at 7.30 a.m. Soon after, they were called by the Stirling pilot who said they were out of position in the stream. They were actually leading when they should be at number eleven. Sgt Fleming and his co-pilot, Sgt Edwards, suggested that the Stirling pilot should simply throttle back and reduce speed, but he insisted on doing a 360 degree turn so that he could re-join the stream in the correct position. The Stirling lost about a thousand feet in this manoeuvre and when it resumed straight and level flight the tow rope between the two aircraft was very slack. There was a severe jerk as the slack was taken up.

The combination of Stirling and glider flew on well until

approaching the English Channel, when the Stirling pilot informed the glider crew that he would join the Great Dunmow stream on the port side. Sgt Fleming told him it was not a good idea, as they would be hit by the slipstream of the Dunmow aircraft. In total there were 1,200 gliders and their 'tugs' (Stirling or Halifax bombers), 200 Dakotas and 200 Liberators – a formidable assembly of aircraft. The Stirling pilot disregarded the advice and began to change position. Soon after, as predicted, the Stirling was hit by the slipstream and rapidly lost 1,500 feet. When it finally straightened out the tow rope was draped between the two aircraft. When the slack was once more taken up, the rope snapped and the glider headed in free flight for the Channel.

As the descent began, Sgt Fleming reminded God in prayer of His promise: 'The eternal God is thy refuge and underneath are the everlasting arms'. He then instructed the corporal to take the inboard axe and cut the escape hatches in the glider's fuselage.

The two pilots flew the Horsa in a fast descent to the top of the sea and levelled off until the tail touched the water. As the drag of the water took hold, the nose of the Horsa plunged into the sea, smashing the cockpit and flooding the fuselage. After some splashing around, everyone managed to get out on to the glider's wing. The aircraft was sinking slowly and they were soon waist deep in the water. Not long after they were rescued by ASR Launch 174 based at Ramsgate. They were given dry clothes and taken to a hospital in Dover for a check-up. Sgt Fleming, with a cut knee, was the only person injured. Finally they were accommodated in Dover Castle.

That evening there was a reunion with the Ox & Bucks soldiers who had been in the glider. The aircrew were told that the corporal who was instructed to cut the escape hatches had, in fact, been trying to hack his way through a small duct in the roof of the Horsa when one of his mates warned him that the duct carried the glider's controls to elevator, ailerons and rudder and that 'the pilots were using them just at present'.

After the war William Fleming became an area manager with George Wimpey & Co. and subsequently a director with Bovis Homes of Scotland. His co-pilot, Sgt Edwards, was eventually to become Chief Superintendent of Police in Wrexham.

Crew of ASR Launch 174:
Harold Wiltshire, Stan Clark, George Dewar and Frank
Ingleton.

JOBS FOR THE GRIMSBY BOYS

One tribute to the men of the Air Sea Rescue Service appeared in the *Grimsby Evening Telegraph* in 1992:

'Grimsby was once the base of the strangest collection of men in the Royal Air Force – they all went to sea. They were the members of No. 22 Air Sea Rescue Squadron, which spent most of the last war operating from the basin outside the lock pits at Grimsby Docks.

'And most of their original complement of men was actually drawn from the Grimsby area. The majority were young recruits who volunteered for an air force which was bursting at the seams with men, so, rather than send them home to wait for vacancies in other branches, the RAF simply posted them to their home town and its three high-speed rescue launches.

'One of their members was Leo Chapman, living in Humberston. No. 22 Air Sea Rescue Squadron was formed in June, 1940, at Gosport and moved to Grimsby in October that year. Mr Chapman was among its original members and remained in his home town until April, 1941, when he was posted to the Far East where he narrowly escaped capture in Singapore.

'His connections with 22 ASR Squadron didn't end there. After service in the Far East he was posted back to Grimsby to await demobilization.

'The squadron was credited with saving the lives of many airmen, particularly in the later stages of the war when activity from the Lincolnshire and Yorkshire bomber airfields reached its height. One launch was always kept on standby in the dock basin with its crew aboard ready to go to the rescue of any aircraft in trouble.

'During Mr Chapman's period, rescues were few and far

between but he recalls his launch picking up a German airman off Spurn. Another launch, sent to look for the crew of a ditched aircraft, came across three other airmen who had been in a dinghy for more than three days. Those men later returned to Grimsby to thank the men who saved their lives just by chance.

'The petrol-engined launches were very fast but had limited reliability and could only operate at high speed in perfect conditions. The Grimsby base covered a wide area of the North Sea and on one occasion in 1941 one launch, under the command of Flt-Lt John Symone, once Grimsby's Port Health Officer, went inside the German minefields to pick up the crew of a ditched bomber off the Terschelling Bank only a few miles from the Dutch coast. It may have been this incident which John Harris referred to in his famous post-war novel *The Sea Shall Not Have Them*.

'The squadron's reserve base was handily placed for access for the crews to both the Oberon and the Barrel public houses. In fact, it was men from 22 ASR Squadron who were among the first on the scene when the Oberon was bombed by a German aircraft in February, 1941.

'The petrol-engined launches were later replaced by slower, but more reliable, diesel-powered vessels which were in service until the end of the war.'

Prior to the arrival of HSLs at Grimsby, there had been *ad hoc* facilities provided by the many trawlers which sailed from the port. One of the earliest reported successes was the rescue of the crew of a No.9 Squadron Wellington bomber on 18 December, 1939.

This aircraft had been carrying out a reconnaissance and an attack on the German fleet at Wilhelmshaven. Flown by one Sgt Ramshaw, the Wellington suffered repeated attacks by ME 110s and sustained extensive damage to the main fuel tanks, leaving only thirty minutes' flying time on reserve tanks.

The Wellington was forced to ditch in the North Sea, about 400 yards from the Grimsby trawler *Erillus*, Sgt Ramshaw having spotted the vessel ahead of the aircraft as the engines died. The rear gunner had been critically wounded and was lost with the aircraft, but the *Erillus* picked up the remaining five crew members and landed them at Grimsby.

From early 1942 the crews of the ASR launches were billeted in two large houses in Abbey Road. The ground floor of one house was used as the Mess, with the cookhouse at the rear. The front room of the second house was a recreation area, with tables and chairs, books and a record player. Other recreational facilities were provided by various churches, cinemas and dance halls. Spencer Capper, who served with the squadron from 1942 to 1944, remembers the morale-boosting efforts of the various organizations, and in particular the kindness and hospitality of a Mr Robson of the School of Art. He taught Spencer the art of woodcarving and offered every encouragement to an 18-year-old who was away from home for the first time. Friendships were also made between crew members and the Abbey Road families; particularly popular were the young ladies at the Abbey Laundry.

The ASR unit operated two types of high speed launches: the Type Two 63-foot 'Whaleback' and the Type Three 68-foot 'Hants & Dorset'. Both vessels had been designed and built by the British Power Boat Company; the nickname 'Whaleback' was given to the Type Two by crews who were impressed by its racy lines and high speed. The Type Three was designed to overcome the shortcomings of the Type Two; it provided better accommodation and an increased range. It was dubbed 'Hants & Dorset' because its rather top-heavy appearance was likened to the South Coast Bus Company's double-decker bus.

One crewman posted to Grimsby after three years' service in Aden and a coxswain's course at Calshot was Wally Bramhall. He spent his first three months with 22 ASR Squadron as NCO in charge of bicycles!

Mr F. Hanson of Bradford served at Grimsby in 1942/43 and remembers HSL 131 colliding with a tug, *The Flying Dutchman*, in the entrance to the outer harbour. The HSL naturally came off worst and lost its bows. Repairs were carried out by base personnel, and the vessel went on to serve at Acklington, Tayport, Littlehampton and Felixstowe before being sunk in the Thames estuary by two Focke-Wulf 190s.

The rescue of six survivors from the crew of a Lancaster is typical of the high degree of co-ordination in ASR. The Lanc had been spotted by an Anson of Coastal Command and HSL 2560 had been scrambled. To ensure success, a second Anson and two

1. **Paddling in the Channel,** *Front row: Left to Right*: George Wilde (navigator);
Norman Bray (pilot); Gord Parkinson (bomb aimer). *Second row:* Les Perkins
(air gunner); Bert Fitchett (wireless operator). *Top:* Dick Stokes (air gunner).
At the time of publication, Bert Fitchett remains a well-known and respected
member of the Goldfish Club Committee.

2. **First Dip for a Halifax,** Charles Harrison's Halifax crew, April, 1942, *Standing Left to Right:* P.O. Dempsey (2nd pilot); Sgt Saunders (navigator); Sgt Oakford (flight engineer); Sgt Charles Harrison (wireless operator); Sgt Wiles (rear gunner). *Front:* W.O. Driscoll (pilot); F/Sgt McLaughlin (wireless operator/mid-upper gunner).

3. **And the Engines Fell Out,** Bombay crew, wearing flying kit: *Left to Right:* Sgt P. Hickling (pilot); P.O. Boast, P.O. Dodds, Sgt Goldsmith (air gunner); Sgt Mark Niman (wireless operator).

4. **Such Language!** John Gibson, DSO, DFC, on the wing of his Hurricane with one of his favourite companions.

5. Six former Battle of Britain pilots, including John Gibson (third from the left), with Edna Munday, organizer of a reunion at Kenley aerodrome in recent years.

6. Sgt Leslie Weddle in 1943.

7. **Sink that Lancaster!** The Lanc that insisted on remaining seaborne.

8. **In a Rubber Ring.** Flight Sergeant Donald M. Kennedy - eight days in the dinghy.

9. **Gardening was no Picnic,** With a Mark III Wellington at Croft in October, 1942. *Left to Right:* Chuck Hancock, Bill Gray, Russ Harling, Gordie Low, Bill McNichol.

10. **Can't Drown, Can't Burn.....**
Airman Reg Edwards with the
Marine Section of the RAF

11. At Middleton St George in June,
1943, with their Halifax. *Left to
Right:* Cliff Wilby, Bill McNichol,
Chuck Hancock

12. **The Girl Who Did a Bleriot.** Gloria's Bleriot replica hits the Channel.

13. Gloria is winched to safety from the submerging aircraft.

14. **When the Bladder was Useful.** Peter Brett and Bill Boorer, crew of the ill-fated Beaufighter. For many years, until his retirement in about 1988, Bill Boorer was the Honorary Treasurer of the Goldfish Club.

15. **Sheilas! - and then there were None.** Crew Eleven at Bassingbourn (11 O.T.U.) in 1942. *Left to Right:* Barney D'ath-Weston (navigator); Bill Frizzell (rear gunner); Lionel Harcus (bomb-aimer/front gunner); Jim Burtt-Smith (pilot); John French (wireless operator).

16. Jim Burtt-Smith in the cockpit of Mark III Wellington at Bassingbourn, 1942...

17. ... and in the cockpit of Wellington bomber salvaged from the bed of Loch Ness
    and under restoration at Brooklands, Surrey (1994).

18. Fifty years on. The four surviving members of Crew 11 at Stratford-on-Avon. *Left to Right:* John French, Lionel Harcus, Jim Burtt-Smith, Barney D'ath Weston.

19. **Floating Kiwis.** Ken Thorn's Catalina sinks into the water while the crew take to the dinghies.

20. The welcome arrival of the high-speed rescue launch.

21. The Catalina crew are welcomed aboard the naval launch.

22, 23, 24. These photos show the rescue of a Whitley bomber crew in 1940 and were taken from the deck of the destroyer *HMS St Mary*. The crew of the Whitley, seen in the third photo, were (clockwise, left to right): Sgt Hird (wireless operator); Sgt Burns (air gunner); Sgt. Collier (co-pilot); P.O. Forsdyke (observer) and in the foreground, F.O. Young (pilot).

American-born Melvyn H. Young ditched twice in 1941 in Whitleys and as a result this very popular rowing blue became known as 'Dinghy' Young. He joined 57 Squadron at Scampton in 1943 for a further tour of 'ops' but was swiftly poached by 617 (Dambusters) Squadron ot become Guy Gibson's deputy. Sadly, returning from the dams raid, his Lancaster was hit by flak and the entire crew were lost in the sea.

25. **A Nasty Little Buoy.** New Zealander Clive Plane in Abu Dhabi in the seventies.

26. Back in New Zealand in 1994.

27. Air Sea Rescue Launches 141 and 142 operating off the coast of North Africa from November, 1941

28. **Compassion.** Canadian businessman George Brown making the presentation to Franz Stigler on behalf of the *Fédération des Combattants Alliés en Europe* (F.C.A.E.E.).

29. The aircraft flown by Charlie Brown and Franz Stigler.

30. The old Air Sea Rescue base at Lyme Regis.

31. The guests at the 1994 reunion.

Hudson aircraft guided the HSL from Spurn Point to the dinghy, 40 miles east of Skegness.

A second rescue illustrates the teamwork existing between the various units. The rescue, in 1941, involved a Whitley bomber which had been hit by night fighters in both engines on its way home from a raid on Berlin. It ditched some 90 miles from the Humber estuary and exploded shortly after the crew had paddled clear in their dinghy, which had overturned in the evacuation. They clung to the upturned dinghy for two days. On the first they were sighted by another Whitley, and on the second by a Hudson, which dropped supplies and flame floats. Further assistance was given on day two by a Hampden bomber, which dropped Lindholme gear, and the crew were finally picked up by a Grimsby-based HSL before nightfall.

Two years later in May, 1943, a Halifax of 102 Squadron was hit by flak over Dortmund and suffered the loss of two engines. It crossed the Dutch coast at 8,000 feet, gradually losing height, and ditched some fifty miles off Spurn Head. All the crew escaped into the dinghy. Early next morning, some three hours later, an ASR Hudson was seen and Very lights were fired. Another hour saw the arrival of two more Hudsons, one of which dropped an airborne lifeboat. The aircrew familiarized themselves with the equipment and started the engine, while the Hudson flashed a course to steer on its Aldis lamp. Initially the aircrew took their own dinghy in tow, but the painter broke and the dinghy was sunk by gunfire from an escorting Hudson. Shortly before noon the escort aircraft lost sight of the lifeboat, which was obscured by low cloud, and the lifeboat also developed engine trouble. The crew rigged up a sail and were eventually seen by a Hudson. ASR launches were given a new course and with assistance from an Anson and a Walrus they located the lifeboat. HSL 2579 picked up the crew and returned to Grimsby. No.22 ASR Squadron continued its important work until December, 1945, and was finally disbanded in August, 1946.

THE LEASE-LEND LAUNCH

Many stories have been told of the rescue of air crews from the sea. These stories, however, are usually told from the airman's point of view. The following account of a sea rescue is told from the rescuer's point of view and shows something of the difficulties and hardships that had to be met and overcome in the course of their normal work by those who man the Air Sea Rescue launches.

The incident described took place between the morning of the 3rd and the afternoon of 6 January, 1943. The rescuers were the crew of HSL 2517 and the rescued were the crew of a Mitchell aircraft of 82 Squadron, USAAF., ditched in the Mediterranean.

The story begins with orders given on the evening of 2 January for HSL 2517 to leave next morning to search for survivors of a crashed aircraft. Everything was made ready and at 0500 the launch left her berth. There was a moderate sea swell and a light wind, but the barometer was falling and there was every indication of an impending storm.

After being stopped twice by patrols off Tobruk, the launch reached the position they had been given and began a square search. This continued for over four hours, but was unavailing. Contact with Tobruk failed, but eventually a message was received from Alexandria which gave a precise position for the dinghy.

The south-westerly wind was now rising, the barometer had fallen and the sky looked threatening. In the early afternoon a Walrus was sighted. The launch made a burst at full speed to attract the pilot's attention with the wake. The Walrus flew over and signalled 'Follow me'. By this time the launch's radio was out of action.

The launch followed the Walrus and, after about half an hour, two dinghies were seen, lashed together. Ten minutes later the launch was alongside and the seven Americans of the Mitchell's crew were hauled aboard with their gear and dinghies. Two were injured and all were stiff and sore after being in the sea for twenty-four hours.

As course was set for Tobruk and the survivors were attended to, the gale was beginning to break. The sea was rising rapidly and the launch began to ship water. Speed had to be dramatically reduced and the first coxswain had to fight hard to keep the vessel's head to wind. By 9 p.m. speed had to be further reduced and after half an hour steerage was lost. She shipped another heavy sea, dipped her bows completely and carried a great volume of water to the wheelhouse top.

Just after nine-thirty the launch stopped within sight of the searchlights and aircraft beacon at Tobruk, but, with the radio still unserviceable, no contact could be made.

There was now a half-gale blowing and a boisterous sea. The launch lay in the trough; to prevent waves breaking on board, engine oil was spread on the water. During the first night of the gale, when the sea was high, the oil saved the launch from damage, and it continued to be used for the two days following. An oil bag was streamed out from the weather quarter and a cigarette-tin of oil poured into each of the two lavatories every half-hour. Fortunately, there was plenty of engine oil in reserve.

By midnight on 3 January it was evident that the launch was caught in an easterly depression and was drifting north-east at about four knots.

Early on the morning of the 4th two destroyers were seen steaming westward about six miles away, but all efforts to contact them visually were unsuccessful. Daylight came with fierce squalls; from noon the wind finally settled to the west and the barometer rose a little. The use of oil was continued carefully as a new sea arose from the west, with waves about eighteen feet from peak to trough.

The morning of 5 January found the sea moderating slightly, although there was still a heavy cross-sea and occasional squally showers. When the sun broke through the wet gear of the crew and the airmen was hung up on the rails to dry. Soon after 3 p.m. a Wellington was spotted, but once again contact could not be made.

The sea continued to moderate; by evening the barometer had risen and remained steady. The use of oil was discontinued.

At 5 a.m. on 6 January the launch's engines were started and it headed south. It ran well before the swell and speed was increased. By 07.20, in first daylight, land was sighted about four miles ahead. After checking the position, course was set for Bardia.

By nine o'clock the launch was off Bardia and fifty minutes later was moored in the harbour. The master went ashore to obtain medical assistance and to inform Tobruk what had happened. The MO and the ambulance arrived and took away the rescued aircrew.

The launch was re-fuelled and prepared for its return to Tobruk, which was reached just after 4 p.m.

Thus an adventure that must have caused the master great anxiety had ended satisfactorily. He reported that all the crew behaved well, although many had been sick. A comment by one of the airmen possibly epitomized what most of them had felt. 'Say, Skip,' he said on the second day at sea, 'if I ever get back to terra firma I'll go down on bended knees and kiss the earth.' Another crew member, when told that the launch was American-built and might be only 'lease-lend', replied, 'Well, you needn't pay for this one; we'll write and tell our President to chalk it right off!'

WHAT GREMLIN?

Lancaster 'Q' for Queenie of 12 Squadron stood at dispersal on a cold, cloudy morning in October, 1944. She was a veteran of more than 20 'ops' and was fully laden that morning with fuel, a 4000-lb 'cookie' and many cans of 4-lb incendiaries which were due to be deposited on the German city of Duisburg.

The seven crew members stood in the shadow of the aircraft, enjoying a last cigarette before take-off, and discussing the topics most popular with young aircrew – mainly wine, women and song.

The wireless operator, F/Sgt Penrose, suddenly looked up at the overcast sky and remarked, 'What a lovely day for a ditching.' The bomb aimer, Flying Officer Norman Chesson, also looked up. To this day he maintains that he saw a little 'gremlin' sitting on the main plane next to the port outer engine with a sardonic smile on its face. As he turned to tell his colleagues, it flew off. Naturally enough, they did not believe him.

Take-off time arrived at 06.40 and once again Queenie thundered down the runway. Soon after lift-off, however, the port outer engine caught fire and could not be extinguished.

Queenie was still too low for the crew to bale out, and with so many small villages below it would not be possible to jettison the bomb load: a 'cookie' could explode even when dropped on 'safe'.

With Queenie now looking more like a comet than a Lancaster, the pilot headed for the coast, while the wireless operator maintained a running commentary with base.

As soon as the Lancaster crossed the coast between Mablethorpe and Saltfleet the bombs were jettisoned; they had been set 'safe' but nevertheless there was an almighty explosion as the 'cookie' hit the water. Quite a few windows were shattered that morning.

By now the port wing was blazing furiously and Queenie, with so many 'ops' behind her, was struggling for height like the tired old lady she was. The New Zealand pilot, Flying Officer C. Henry, skilfully brought the aircraft down on to a rather rough North Sea, and the fire was extinguished. Queenie broke her back and began to sink very quickly.

The crew had already taken up ditching positions and Norman Chesson released the pilot's escape hatch. He grasped whatever he could to stabilize himself but as Queenie hit the water he was ejected into the nose of the aircraft. All the crew got out safely into the dinghy and watched as Queenie sank beneath the waves in less than a minute.

The cloud base was very low – only a few hundred feet – but after about an hour the dinghy was spotted by an ASR Hudson. Shortly afterwards ASR launch 2578, skippered by Flying Officer Kirkland, arrived on the scene and the airmen were returned to Grimsby. With the rest of the crew, Norman Chesson was given a tot of Navy rum; it was very good, he says, but made him very sick.

Later that morning the crew were transported back to Wickenby, to be informed that their very hazardous flight of 30 minutes would be counted as an operation to add to their number of completed missions. Over 1,000 aircraft had taken part in that morning's raid and Queenie was the first to be lost.

Norman Chesson says he is now the sole survivor of his crew, but each year on 14 October he wishes them well, wherever they may be. He says 'hello' to that gremlin as well.

HOME IS A HIGH-SPEED LAUNCH

Flying Officer Len Cullingford returned to the U.K. early in 1944 after three years of sun, sand and flies and was posted to 512 Squadron of 46 Group. His heart sank when he learned that the squadron was engaged on paratroop dropping and glider towing. Dicey, he thought. How right he was.

On the night of 5/6 June, 1944, southern England reverberated to the roar of countless aircraft passing overhead, including those of 38 and 46 Groups conveying glider-borne troops and paratroops of the 6th Airborne Division to Normandy with specific tasks to carry out before the main beach landings on D-Day. During the night the Merville coastal gun battery was put out of action and what is now known as 'Pegasus Bridge' was taken. Len Cullingford continues the story:

'The evening of D-Day, 6 June, saw 250 Dakotas, Stirlings and Halifaxes from 38 and 46 Groups towing an equal number of gliders, Horsas and Hamilcars, with reinforcement troops, ammunition, jeeps, light guns and tanks. For reasons unknown, 512 Squadron had been appointed lead squadron, and as I was navigator to the Officer Commanding (Flying), Squadron Leader Rae, I found myself in the Dakota which led the whole formation.

'As we approached land at about 2,000 feet I had an uninterrupted view of what was going on below on the beaches. It was like looking down on a stage from the front row of the Grand Circle: the Navy offshore, the landing craft, the smoke and flame of battle and, as a backcloth, the town of Caen going up in smoke. It was an awe-inspiring and frightening sight. The sky above was solid with fighter aircraft.

'Having released our Horsa glider at 800 feet over the dropping

71

zone near Pegasus Bridge, we descended to 500 feet to release the tow rope, hoping it might clobber some Germans. Soon after, however, there was the unwelcome sound of metal hitting our aircraft; flying so low, we were an easy target. Squadron Leader Rae 'jinked' the Dakota like mad, but the enemy had knocked out the starboard engine and inflicted other damage. We staggered away on one engine and back across the French coast.

'I had been shot in both legs and a large chunk of metal had passed through my left arm, but it was still mobile. Before much longer the port engine gave up the ghost and we had to ditch.

'Landing on the sea was a totally new experience. As we splashed down, water washed right over the Dakota but fortunately its buoyancy was sufficient to bring us up and afloat. Fortunately, too, our dinghy pack had not been damaged and the dinghy inflated steadily as we threw it out into the sea. Out we went, one after the other: pilot, co-pilot, wireless operator and me, into this fragile 6-foot diameter open rubber dinghy. It was by no means easy, as there was quite a heavy swell and the dinghy was heaving up and down in the water. At least we were safe for the time being, but somewhat anxious as we drifted away helplessly.

'Although we did not know it, help was not far away. Because of all the unusual air activity, several ASR launches had been stationed across the Channel. One of these had seen us go down, and to our joy, after about half-an-hour of gloom and anxiety, we saw first the masthead, then the hull of a rescue launch racing towards us. How our mood changed, and how relieved we were to leave that dinghy for something more solid and secure.

'By now it was growing dark. The skipper of the launch decided that the safest thing would be to spend the night with the invasion fleet, as it was possible that on the open sea we might be mistaken for a German E-boat.

'It was a noisy night: any movement, imagined or real, brought a burst of fire. At dawn we moved off back across the Channel. By now my legs had seized up and I had to be carried off into an ambulance when we reached Southampton. In hospital I had sundry bits of metal removed from my legs and left arm, but no lasting damage had been done. Once again, I had been extremely lucky.

'I should mention that while we were lying off the French beaches after dark with the invasion fleet, we saw some of our own aircraft shot down by the ever trigger-happy Royal Navy. They were Dakotas of our own and sister Squadrons of 46 Group, on a re-supply mission to the 6th Airborne, carrying under-slung canisters of petrol and ammunition to be dropped by parachute. Another of those tragedies of war.'

Len Cullingford and his fellow crew members were rescued by HSL 2561. One of the fitters on that vessel was LAC Basil Kain, who has given his own account of the incident.
'We left Calshot at about 6 a.m. on D-Day and made full speed with hundreds of other ships and landing craft. We first covered the area of 'Gold' beach, but in the afternoon we were directed to the Le Havre area. The sea was rather choppy, but 2561 was moving at full speed when the wireless operator, Sgt Cameron, shouted down the engine room hatch that an aircraft towing a glider had ditched. (Sgt Cameron, incidentally, was officially attached to base signals, but had 'stowed away' on 2561; he did not want to miss D-Day!) The engines slowed, the coxswain controlled the launch's speed, and we were soon alongside a dinghy. The pick-up was made. Attempts were made by wireless to find a hospital ship in the beachhead area so that the casualties could be transferred, but we had no success. One of the crew we had picked up was in a bit of a mess [Mr Cullingford] and the medical orderly was worried about his condition, but the skipper, Flying Officer Bond, had dished out a good helping of rum to the rescued aircrew.
   'Down in the engine room I was only aware that 2561 was back in the assault area, where we stayed the night. I believe we did try to break out during the night but were fired on by destroyers. An HSL looks very like an E-boat in the dark. Rather a worried night was had by all.
   'At first light, however, it was full speed for the South Coast. When in mid-Channel the speed slowed and I was informed by A.C. Russell that another dinghy had been spotted. This turned out to contain a Canadian fighter pilot who had been in the drink for three days and was in rather a bad way. He said he had seen all the aircraft flying over in the two days before D-Day and since, but no one had sighted him. The medical orderly, LAC Brooksbank, told us that apart from exposure and hypothermia he was all right. I understand he made a full recovery.

'Once again we made full speed and saw the cliffs of the Seven Sisters near Eastbourne. I thought the skipper would make for Newhaven, where there was an ASR base, but he decided (or was ordered) to go to Calshot, where ambulances and medical staff were waiting to deal with our pick-ups.

'HSL 2561 operated from Mulberry Harbour at Arromanches until moving to Ostend in August for operations along the Belgian, French and Dutch coasts. At the end of the war 33 ASR was posted to Norway, with two boats at Oslo, two at Bergen and two at Stavanger. HSL 2561 was based at Trondheim until November, 1945.'

'When I got divorced,' wrote Babs Ludlam, 'I decided to get away from it all and, after much searching, found the perfect home – a sweet little houseboat moored on a sleepy backwater.

'I moved in and started to decorate. The more work I did, the more I started to wonder about its history. All I knew was that it had been converted into a houseboat 30 years ago.

'I then discovered my home was an RAF rescue launch during the war. She was officially referred to as Launch 2561, but her crew called her Blue Leader. She often raced into the Channel to save RAF men who'd been shot down. Many times her crew risked their lives under heavy fire. But that was just the half of it. Blue Leader was the actual boat used in the film *The Sea Shall Not Have Them*, starring Dirk Bogarde and Michael Redgrave. The author of the book on which the film was based was a member of the Blue Leader's crew.

'Sadly, he died, but I set out to track down the rest of the crew. I found so many that, last year, on the 50th anniversary of Blue Leader's inaugural voyage, I had a get-together. It was a very emotional occasion because some of the men hadn't seen each other for more than 40 years. I still receive news and photographs of Blue Leader and her sister launches. It's like living with a celebrity, but I feel honoured to be aboard.'

And one final word from Basil Kain:-

'The worst day was 27 August, 1944, when rocket-firing Typhoons sank two Royal Navy minesweepers which had been clearing mines at the entrance to Le Havre, and damaged three others. One hundred and seventeen sailors died, but HSL 2561, which was in the area, picked up over a hundred survivors (all wounded) and put them on a hospital ship in Mulberry Harbour. The remarks of the sailors about being sunk by the RAF and picked up by the RAF were not printable! Medical Orderly Brooksbank should have been awarded a medal for his work that day. HSL 2561 did receive a signal from the Flag Officer, British Assault Areas, congratulating it on its good work.'

Crew of HSL 2561 (D-Day):-
Flying Officer Bond (Captain)
F/Sgt Greenhill (1st coxswain)
Cpl Simpson (2nd coxswain)
Cpl Stewart (motor boat crew)
LAC Lithgow   (ditto)
AC Taylor   (ditto)
AC Russell   (ditto)
LAC Brooksbank (medical orderly)
Sgt Cameron (wireless operator)
Sgt Rundle (fitter)
LAC Kain (fitter)

GARDENING WAS NO PICNIC

It was known by RAF bomber crews as 'gardening' – planting high explosive mines in the shipping channels off the coast of Europe with the object of sinking enemy shipping.

On 27 February, 1943, eight Mark II Halifax bombers took off in the early evening from their base at Middleton St George in Co Durham. They belonged to 419 Royal Canadian Air Force Squadron (the 'Moose' Squadron). Soon after take-off they joined up with twenty-six other bombers and headed for the Frisian Islands, off the Dutch coast, to do that night's 'gardening'.

One of the 419 Squadron bombers was piloted by Sgt M. F. 'Bill' Gray; it would be his 12th operational trip. With him were three members of his original Wellington crew: Sergeants Bill McNichol (bomb-aimer), Chuck Hancock (navigator) and Gordie Low (wireless operator). Completing the crew were three new members – Sergeants Cliff Wilby (flight engineer), Matt Braniff (mid-upper gunner) and F/Sgt Russ Harling (rear gunner). With the exception of Matt Braniff, who hailed from New Orleans, the crew were all Canadian.

The trip across the North Sea to the Frisian Islands went smoothly. The weather was good, but it was very dark as they reached the target area. As the Halifax descended from 6,000 feet, searching for a map reference among the islands, they flew directly over a flak ship at about 1,000 feet. Sure enough, it opened up with light anti-aircraft tracer shells and the Halifax was hit in the port wing. But the aircraft was now on its bombing run and Bill Gray stayed on course and at 500 feet the two 2,000 lb mines were dropped on target.

Climbing away on a heading for base, it was soon obvious that the port inner engine was badly damaged: it had to be feathered.

It was then discovered that the hydraulic system had been damaged. The bomb doors could not be closed, nor could the radiator shutters on the three remaining engines be opened. Fifteen minutes later the port outer engine failed and had to be shut down. By this time the Halifax was down to about 3,000 feet and in order to maintain altitude the starboard engines had to be opened up to nearly full power and soon began to overheat. The aircraft was extremely difficult to control. Flying at less than 1,000 feet, just above stalling speed, Bill Gray ordered the crew to take up ditching positions. Gordie Low sent out an SOS with the plane's position.

At 9 p.m. the Halifax ditched, about 100 miles east of Hull. The crew carried out their drill perfectly. In spite of the dark night the landing was excellent. Gray had discovered that the landing light, in the vertical position, was a big help in judging his distance above the water just before touch-down. At the last minute he jettisoned the escape hatch above his head, at the same time closing the throttles and cutting the switches to the starboard engines.

The Halifax hit the water in a tail-down, wings-level position at about a hundred miles an hour. The second impact a few seconds later was much more severe and brought the aircraft to a stop. Bill Gray lost consciousness for several minutes from the shock of the landing and when he came to he was sitting waist-high in icy water. He climbed out of the hatch. The dinghy had inflated successfully. He had worried about this, since it had been stowed immediately behind the port inner engine, which had been hit by flak.

The crew had already climbed out of the two rear escape hatches and were standing on the semi-submerged port wing, preparing to board the dinghy. It was no easy task to get seven airmen in flying suits, plus emergency equipment and rations and two drowned pigeons in a container, into the small, round rubber dinghy. When they were finally organized and floating away, the Halifax was still afloat.

After a long, wet night the crew were relieved to see two friendly aircraft circling overhead. Owing to some mix-up however, they were not picked up until seven o'clock that evening, when two RAF rescue launches appeared on the horizon. The crew were taken to a Naval Hospital at Grimsby and, after a short stay, they returned by train to Middleton St George to continue their operational tour.

For the rear gunner, Russ Harling, it was a particularly

unwelcome event. Not only was it his second ditching, but he had only just married a WAAF and was officially on leave. As Bill Gray said, 'Just imagine spending your honeymoon in a dinghy in the North Sea with six other guys!'

HERE'S YOUR TROUSERS, GEORGE

During the Second World War there was often a certain degree of resentment expressed by British aircrews towards their Commonwealth counterparts. Admittedly, these young men from Australia, Canada, New Zealand and other far corners of the earth had a different temperament; more volatile, less amenable to discipline, they were nevertheless equally courageous and dedicated to the tasks they had travelled so far to undertake. So why did the friction exist between British aircrew and their Commonwealth colleagues, sometimes referred to by the more politically incorrect as 'those bloody Colonials'?

Perhaps there is a clue contained in the report of Flight Sergeant Bern Battis, operating as wireless operator/air gunner in Hampden bombers from Bircham Newton (Norfolk) in 1943. His pilot was P.O. Harry Parkinson; P.O. Tom Fettes was navigator and F/Sgt George Lindsay (WOP/AG) completed the crew. Three were Australians; George Lindsay was a Canadian.

Sunday, 18 July, 1943, began like any other operational morning – a call-out at around 3.30 a.m., a leisurely walk to the mess for breakfast, a call at the Flight Room where the navigator collected some gear before arriving at the operations room for briefing.

Now let Bern Battis continue the story:

'We were picked up by transport after briefing and taken back to the Flight Room to pick up our Mae Wests and parachutes, etc. George and I had an arrangement with some of the girls in the M.T. (motor transport) Section to do a bit of ironing for us, and we had brought up a pair of trousers each to be ironed to make us look presentable at the Sergeants' Mess dance that night. The

M.T. driver that morning was new, so we showed her the lockers the trousers were to be put in when ready.'

Well, there you are. These Commonwealth lads seemed to be able to *get away* with things which to the more reserved and diffident English nature would seem like taking a liberty. In any case, it is highly doubtful if many English aircrew ironed their trousers in preparation for a dance, unless they had been on leave and mum had been particularly sympathetic. It is to be hoped that the M.T. girls got some sort of reward, or shouldn't we ask?

When Bern Battis and his crew reached the aircraft that morning, there was the usual banter with the ground staff, who said how well they had serviced the Hampden and what a fine job they had done. The aircraft took off at 5.50 a.m.

This was to be one of the regular meteorological flights carried out each morning, heading away from Bircham Newton at 030 degrees for 300 nautical miles, taking temperature readings, cloud types and wind speed (if possible) every 50 miles. At distances of 150 miles and 300 miles a descent was made to sea level to get the barometric pressure at those points. The Hampden's normal cruising speed was 150 knots and the outward journey would therefore take about two hours.

After the descent to sea level at the 300 mile point, a climb was made to reach a barometric pressure of 950 millibars – generally in the region of 15,000 feet – and thereafter taking readings every fifty millibars, levelling off at each stage to allow the instruments to settle down and give reasonably accurate readings. The climb lasted for about 30 minutes; then the aircraft headed 'downhill' for Bircham Newton.

At about 8.15 a.m. on that morning, when the Hampden was flying at about 11,000 feet on the ascent, the starboard engine failed. Since the aircraft was not very far from the Norwegian coast, there was a brief discussion among the crew as to whether they should try to get to Sweden or head back for home. No one had any information about the height of the mountains they would have to cross on the Scandinavian peninsula and it was agreed that they should try to reach base.

Bircham Newton was notified by high frequency radio that the Hampden was in trouble and the nature of the trouble was described. Permission was then requested to change to medium frequency in order that Bircham Newton's direction finders could pinpoint the Hampden's position. This was done.

It was fortunate that Bircham Newton was the control station for the East Coast medium frequency direction-finding group of stations. Moreover, two Air Sea Rescue Squadrons were based there: 280 Squadron, flying Ansons, and 281 Squadron equipped with Hudsons. These were alerted to stand by in case they were needed. The Hampden's wireless operator sent a transmission every five minutes, giving the aircraft's height and the course being flown.

Since the propellor on the starboard engine could not be fully feathered, it was simply 'windmilling' and creating a fair amount of drag on the plane. It was hard work for the pilot. On only one engine and with the added drag, the Hampden was gradually losing height, even though the pilot was trying to maintain a reasonable speed.

By about 10 o'clock the aircraft was down to 1,000 feet. Suddenly the pilot momentarily lost control and the Hampden went briefly into a spin and about 400 feet were lost. Two minutes later its height was down by another 400 feet. The pilot realized there was now no alternative to ditching, so George Lindsay sent out an SOS and the crew assumed their ditching positions.

As far as the weather was concerned it was as near a perfect day as could be wished for. There was a thin layer of broken cloud at about 6,000 feet, but nothing beyond. From peak to trough the waves were about four feet high. Harry Parkinson put the aircraft down very gently along the side of a trough and the landing was relatively smooth. The crew suffered no bruises, scratches or broken bones. A perfect ditching.

Having an unimpeded exit, the pilot was first out of the aircraft, followed quickly by Tom Fettes, Bern Battis and George Lindsay. The crew were all clear of the aircraft in little more than five seconds. The 'H' type dinghy stowed in the engine nacelle had opened automatically and inflated right side up; the pilot and navigator pushed it away from the wing and climbed aboard. Battis and Fettes were trying to stow extra Very cartridges and a pistol into their flying gear and take an extra 'K' type dinghy with them. When they turned around, their two colleagues were already about 40 yards away from the Hampden, so they inflated their Mae Wests, stepped off the wing of the aircraft and drifted down to join the others, who slowed the dinghy's progress. The gear was transferred to the main dinghy, the 'K' type was inflated and the two late-comers joined their companions.

They all settled down patiently for a rescue, knowing that they were inside the convoy line and were bound to see plenty of aircraft. Sure enough, after only ten minutes a Lancaster flew over-head at about 1,500 feet, but failed to see the signal flares. A few minutes later came another Lancaster, about two miles distant, but there was still no response. Finally, after they had been in the water for just under an hour, the crew saw a Hudson of 281 Squadron bearing down on them. This aircraft dropped a smoke float from about a hundred feet and then went into the drill of climbing to approximately 5,000 feet and transmitting the position in order that their signal would be received clearly at base. No more than fifteen minutes later there were six Ansons of 280 Squadron buzzing over the dinghy, followed by the Commanding Officer, Squadron Leader Bispham, in a Gladiator.

The Hudson, which had flown away after its climb, then returned and dropped another float from a great height, which slightly unnerved the airmen in the dinghy. It then signalled that a trawler was on its way. Some time later the crew saw thick, black smoke on the horizon. It was an old coal-burner. As the vessel drew closer the smoke could be seen belching out and the crew felt great sympathy for the stokers. It crawled towards them and held their attention, until one of the crew looked the other way and saw an Air Sea Rescue launch arriving at a rate of knots.

It was Launch 2579 from Immingham. They picked up the Hampden crew at 12.35 p.m., took them back to Immingham and provided transport to an airfield near North Coates. Soon after, the CO arrived in an Anson borrowed from 280 Squadron and they were flown back to Bircham Newton.

After they had been de-briefed in the Operations Room, the Intelligence Officer asked, 'What happened to the pigeons?' He was told that it had been impossible to retrieve them and that they had gone down with the aircraft. He appeared to be somewhat put out, and murmured something to the effect that the RAF would have to pay the pigeon owner five shillings for each bird. Two of the crew offered to pay, but this was declined. Bern Battis thought the officer was annoyed at the prospect of the reams of paperwork involved in the loss of the pigeons.

After drinks with the CO in the Officers' Mess, the crew repaired to the flight rooms where Battis and Lindsay collected their immaculately-pressed trousers.

As an afterthought, Bern Battis remarks that both 280 and 281 Squadrons had previously had a pretty bleak time searching for dinghies until the rescue of the Hampden crew. This may be the reason for the appearance of no fewer than six Ansons after the Hudson had spotted them, or maybe their CO wanted them to see what a dinghy in the water really looked like. In the ensuing weeks, however, both Squadrons were very busy and took part in a number of rescues.

CAN'T DROWN, CAN'T BURN

When he joined the Royal Air Force in the Second World War it was never the intention of Corporal Reg Edwards to go to sea. As a wireless operator mechanic, he was a member of an emergency party based at RAF West Drayton. They would await orders to proceed to any destination and deal with any problems related to his trade. During the early days of the war, this involved work on such bomber aircraft as Fairey Battles, Herefords, Hampdens, Whitleys and Wellingtons, in which wireless equipment was installed, modified and repaired.

Now we can let Reg tell the rest of his story:

'With the occupation of Iceland, a party of wireless mechanics was despatched forthwith to that country to erect aerial systems in order that a transmitting station could be put into operation.

'Our trip in an American Catalina flying boat took about seven hours. The journey was quite uneventful, in spite of a violent thunderstorm. We flew almost at wavetop level to prevent any attack from below by enemy planes, as the Catalina was very vulnerable from that direction. Not until we landed on the sea in Reykjavik bay did I learn to my dismay that I was no sailor, and the trip ashore in a Norwegian tender confirmed this.

'My return home was aboard an Irish packet boat, the *Leinster*. Its zigzag course through heavy seas left me legless – a total wreck. I lay on a lower deck for the next five days. At one time I tried a hammock, but with no success. Just how bad I felt is underlined by the fact that no food passed my lips during the entire journey. I was not even aroused from my misery by a U-boat attack and the ensuing battle, which ended when our destroyer escort drove it off.

'I returned to Iceland for a further spell of duty on a fair-sized troopship. This had been a South African liner, the *Llanstephan Castle*. I thanked God that it was a reasonably smooth passage. The only incident of note was being rammed in thick fog, during the night, by our lease-lend four-funnel destroyer escort. There was little damage, although a number of airmen were thrown from their bunks.

'Preparing for my final return to the U.K., I stood on the dockside sizing up the liner standing offshore. Here was a ship, I thought, worthy of a smooth journey home. A pinnace took us alongside. We climbed aboard and were met by a Flight Sergeant, who ordered us to cross the deck and climb down to the ship moored alongside. Yes, it was none other than the *Leinster*.

'To add insult to injury the *Leinster* sailed north to pick up troops in the Arctic who were also returning to Britain. This added two more days to our journey. Once again I was sea-sick during the whole trip, unable to eat a single meal and swearing that if it were humanly possible I would never travel on the sea again. Anyone who has suffered the soul-destroying effects of *mal-de-mer* will confirm how distressing the experience can be. The only thought coursing through the mind is "Stop the ship, I want to get off." Yet once again, we had a safe journey.

'Returning home on a week's leave, I remember that not even my own mother recognised the gaunt, dishevelled figure standing before her on the doorstep. But one week at home soon put the colour back into my cheeks.

'On my return to base, I was met by an officer who recognized me from pre-war days; we had both worked at the H.M.V. factory at Hayes. I had just been promoted to Corporal and he said he thought I was just the chap he was looking for. Foolishly, I failed to ask any questions about the section I was joining. After a year and a half in Iceland I thought it would be good to have a change.

'So it was that I found myself on attachment to a Marine Section of the RAF, due to spend the following year on high-speed launches and fast Naval launches. Initially, my stomach turned over at the mere thought of returning to sea. Such thoughts, in fact, were well founded on missions involving "laying to" off Dungeness or in mid-Channel, to rendezvous with Flying Fortresses returning from bombing raids on the continent. Many of my trips finished in this manner.

'Although I was not an official crewman, while aboard there were many occasions when I would hear the starter cartridges fire the three Napier aero engines. They would roar into life, ropes would be cast off and the launch would head off on yet another mercy mission. I did enjoy the experience of bouncing across the waves at high speed until the order was given: "Stop all engines". If there was a heavy sea running, the effect of wallowing soon reduced me once again to the most wretched condition.

'It is strange to relate that during all those trips over a period of twelve months I never witnessed the saving of a single soul from the sea. At the same time, however, I am glad to say that on no occasion did we sight a German E-boat or R-boat. I understand they would have had no compunction about blowing us out of the water. A number of boats were reputedly sunk in this way.

'It should be remembered that these rescue launches were intended solely for "mercy missions" and were consequently poorly armed, with only Vickers light machine guns for defence purposes. These were absolutely no match for the heavily-armed German E-boats and R-boats. It later became necessary to re-arm our launches with twin Brownings in the turrets and a 20 mm Oerlikon cannon aft, giving them a little more protection. The launches were also attacked occasionally by German FW 190 fighters.

'My year on the sea was divided into equal periods on RAF launches and Naval craft, and took me to bases along the entire length of the South Coast, from Ramsgate and Dover to Newlyn (Cornwall) and the Scilly Isles. But I never gained my sea legs.

'It was during one of my spells at the Newhaven HSL base, in preparation for the raid on Dieppe, that I had two narrow escapes. One day I leapt aboard an HSL moored alongside the quay. I missed my footing and fell between the launch and the quayside. By sheer good fortune I managed to clutch a gun stanchion. Had I fallen, I may well have drowned, since I was a non-swimmer. Meanwhile, the launch was gently swaying to and fro against the quay and could easily have crushed me. As it was, I struggled to swing sideways to gain a foothold on the deck – not an easy task, because of the cut-away hull. In sheer panic I managed by some means to drag myself aboard and I was happy to know that I would not lose my life by accident as opposed to enemy action.

'Soon after this incident I was engaged in coupling a cable to the mains DC supply box. This was sited in the cramped conditions of the launch's engine room, where the bulkhead lighting was not particularly good. Straining my eyes to see where the cable entered the box, I failed to notice that a live "busbar" was not bolted firmly in place. It dropped suddenly on to a lug underneath and short-circuited. There was a fearsome flash which momentarily blinded me. On regaining my sight, I was horrified to see that the flash had ignited a small amount of petrol which was trapped in the channelling riveted to the hull. Three other airmen who had been with me disappeared up through the hatch like greased lightning, their feet echoing across the deck above and then along the quayside, where, from a respectable distance, they awaited events. I didn't blame them. I had once seen the effect of fire on a launch that was being refuelled at Portsmouth; nothing had been left but floating driftwood. Fortunately, on this occasion I was wearing my hat, which I used to smother the fire before it gained a hold. As I reappeared on deck a cheer went up from the lads on the quayside. I was uncertain whether it was meant for me or for the launch. After that escapade I made sure that I learned how to swim.

'Another incident caused me some anxiety at the time. Once again, it happened in the engine room. My blueprints were spread out on the table below the hatch when an airman armourer poked his head through and asked, "Is Joe down there?" A live 20 mm cannon shell dropped out of the top pocket of his dungarees and fell on to the table in front of me. The red nose of the shell told me that it had an explosive head, and I had been told that they exploded on impact. With a few choice words, I handed it back to him. Five minutes later the same head appeared in the hatch, still calling for Joe. The very same shell virtually parted my hair. This time I read him the Riot Act before he disappeared. It may be hard to believe, but the same performance was repeated a third time, but on that occasion the shell went straight overboard instead of being returned to its owner. There were no words; my face must have said it all. I never saw that airman again. Perhaps he should have been put on a charge, but I never did that during my entire service.

'I seem to remember that during the Dieppe raid in the summer of 1942 two of our launches failed to return to base, destroyed by enemy action.

'Dover was an active base, but once again I was fortunate. The greatest danger arose from the long-range German artillery, which was shelling Dover from the French port of Calais. At that time I was billeted in the annexe to the Lord Warden Hotel. Only a week after my return to base in London the annexe received a direct hit from one of those massive shells. On the sea front at Dover there is a plaque reminding residents and visitors of those unhappy days. Few people appreciate that, as the citizens of London were plagued by the V1 and V2 missiles, so the good people of Dover suffered constantly from the arrival of those high explosive shells from over the Channel.

'During my stay at Dover, operating aboard Naval launches, I noticed that many Naval ratings were tattooed with Naval emblems. As a member of the RAF I decided to be different, and was tattooed with a pair of wings. Age has taken its toll and it is now only a faded image of its original red and blue glory, but still a reminder of stirring days.

'Also at Dover, I heard of one RAF launch which had just rescued a ditched aircrew when it became enveloped in dense fog. Not far away they could hear the sound of at least one other diesel engine accompanied by guttural German commands. The HSL shut down its engines. After remaining silent for a considerable time, the engines were restarted and given full throttle; the launch made a high-speed escape, followed by streams of tracer. Apparently the Germans had also been playing a waiting game.

'There is one final tale of woe. This event happened in the Scilly Isles with the landing of a Sunderland flying boat in the sea in St Mary's Bay. I had never boarded – or even seen – one of these huge aircraft before. I simply had to have a closer look at her. Borrowing a dinghy and an oar, I sculled out into the bay to gaze in awe at this truly majestic plane-cum-boat. It was gently rocking from port to starboard on a reasonably calm sea. On my second circuit around this giant there was suddenly a startling crash beside my dinghy. I had completely overlooked the fact that an enormous float was mounted beneath each wing of the Sunderland; one float rested on the water while the other was held high on the opposite wing, and in the gentle swell the two floats changed position.

Inadvertently I had paddled almost underneath the raised float, which had then crashed down no more than two feet from the dinghy. But then I was young and inexperienced and only had myself to blame for what could have been a fatal accident.'

WHEN THE BLADDER WAS USEFUL

The eleventh hour of the eleventh day of the eleventh month – that was the moment when the First World War came to an end. The massacre of hundreds of thousands of young men in the fields of Northern France was finally over. We have doubtless all heard stories of sons, husbands and fathers who lost their lives only minutes, maybe seconds before that fateful hour.

The next ditching story is a reminder of what may happen in that narrow interval between war and peace. It is told by W. G. (Bill) Boorer, who was a navigator on a Beaufighter flown by Peter Brett.

'After a briefing on Thursday, 3 May, 1945, the Dallachy wing of "Torbeau" anti-shipping strike aircraft flew off from Dallachy for a major strike against a large fleet of enemy shipping which was assembling in Kiel Bay. Intelligence had suggested that the Germans were intending to escape to Norway and continue the war from there.

'Peter Brett and I were one of the crews on the wing with the longest experience and we were therefore appointed as the "outrider" – the aircraft which would fly ahead of the main strike force, select the best targets and direct the strike force on to those targets.

'We flew on ahead on a "flak free" route across Denmark, selected by the 2nd Tactical Air Force, and made our landfall at Ringkobing. We were hedge-hopping at full throttle towards the "Little Belt" when we suddenly found ourselves engulfed in flak. We had flown between two batteries of 88 mm anti-aircraft guns.

'Our port engine burst into flame immediately, but our speed and low altitude carried us quickly out of the danger area. Peter turned back for home with the intention of flying back on the starboard engine only. It was not to be. A short while after crossing the coast the remaining engine failed and we had to ditch in the North Sea.

'At the time of ditching the sea was very calm and we had no problems – or so we thought. The dinghy emerged from the port wing and, as a non-swimmer, I jumped into it as it drifted back. Alas, I found it to be as flat as a pancake, having been peppered with holes from the flak which had shot out the port engine during the attack. Pete swam up, the Beaufighter gave a gurgle and disappeared, and we inflated our Mae Wests. We spent what seemed to be hours finding the various holes and sealing them with the adhesive repair patches. Finally we had to inflate the dinghy with the hand pump and clamber aboard, which was not quite as easy as it sounds. Suddenly we remembered the airtight container carrying the emergency rations, which was attached to the dinghy by a tie-line. We saw it was floating a short distance away. As we pulled on the line, however, the container disappeared beneath the waves. Consequently we had no food or water throughout our ditching.

'During the night the weather deteriorated, but on the morning of the second day, 4 May, we were in reasonably good spirits and had every hope of being picked up. For our particular operation Air Sea Rescue Warwick aircraft had been on patrol along the western coast of Denmark and I had managed to send an SOS on my radio set. I learned later, however, that, although my message was actually received, the signal was so weak because of the very low power generated by our one remaining – and failing – engine that the message had been indecipherable. Moreover, we were drifting southwards quite rapidly. In fact, when we were finally rescued we were some 50 miles south of our original ditching position.

'During that second day we heard and caught glimpses of two aircraft and fired off some of our two-star red cartridge signals. But there was no response. In spite of a very heavy sea that night, we were still relatively comfortable.

'On Saturday, 5 May the heavy sea continued throughout the day. In the evening the weather worsened into a heavy storm, with waves up to sixty feet high. Sometimes we were at the bottom of these huge waves and sometimes at the top, like a seaside roller-coaster. During the course of the evening we saw a Liberator some distance away. We fired off our last two-star red which they obviously saw, as they turned and flew right above us and a member of the crew waved to us from the rear door. Unfortunately, the sea was so rough that they lost sight of us almost immediately after, and although we watched them as they continued to circle and search, they gradually moved farther and farther away. And, of course, we had no more two-star reds! During that night we shipped gallons of water. Several of the adhesive repair patches became non-effective and had to be replaced with conical rubber plugs.

'The weather eased slightly during the course of Sunday, but became extremely rough once again that night. We both began to feel the torture of thirst and had to resort to moistening our lips with our own urine – not a very encouraging experience. As the holes in the dinghy grew larger, the conical plugs had to be pushed farther in and eventually had to be replaced with larger sizes. During the day I felt the need to sustain my spirits with a little hymn singing, but I had the feeling that Peter did not really appreciate my efforts.

'By this time, too, my underpants, which were Canadian cotton issue, had shrunk considerably and I was extremely uncomfortable in a very sensitive area. Finally I cast modesty aside and left a certain part of my physical equipment hanging free. Peter described it as looking like the head of a very ancient and wizened tortoise.

'By Monday morning the sea had moderated considerably and by nightfall the wind had dropped. For the first time since our ditching on the previous Thursday it was quite calm. Early in the morning we had fixed a piece of chewing gum to a line and thrown it into the sea in the hope of catching a fish. During the afternoon the dinghy gave a heavy lurch, the fishing line went taut and, sure enough, there was a cod on the hook. Despite our best endeavours to get it aboard, however, it eventually broke free and disappeared. In retrospect, I am not quite sure what we would have done with it had we actually landed it in the dinghy.

'We had entered our fifth day aboard the dinghy feeling pretty weak and we again resorted to urine to stave off the demoralizing effects of thirst. There was a growing apprehension about our future, particularly as the rubber plugs had now progressed to the largest size available and were now inserted well into the holes in the rubber, so that there was little of the plugs remaining for further insertion. Our spirits reached a low ebb.

'As night closed in once more, we became aware of a gradually increasing noise. Eventually a small ship loomed on the horizon. Peter and I discussed whether or not we should attempt to attract its attention, since we had heard reports that the Germans were prone to shooting up any British dinghies that they came across. We finally decided that in view of our deteriorating condition we did not have much option, so we blew our whistles, shouted and waved our hands. The ship, which turned out to be the *Ella*, a fishing boat from Esbjerg, altered course and hove alongside the dinghy.

'Someone leaned over and shouted, "British Tommy?" and on hearing our affirmative he then shouted "Germany *kaput*!" This was the first intimation we had had that Nazi Germany had at last thrown in the towel, in fact on midnight of the day we had ditched.

'Once on board the fishing boat I became somewhat delirious and the skipper, Christian Peterson, turned back to Esbjerg.

'We arrived in Esbjerg fishing harbour during the morning of Tuesday, 8 May, were offloaded and taken by ambulance to the Central Hospital, arriving at about midday on VE Day. One inmate, a victim of Gestapo treatment, sent us in his radio and we listened to the celebrations from Piccadilly.'

TWO LANCS TOO CLOSE

Ken Rimell is the founder and Director of the Museum of D-Day Aviation at Shoreham Airport in Sussex. He has given the following account of the rescue of a Lancaster crew by 29 Air Sea Rescue Unit in 1943. It is reprinted by kind permission of *Bomber Command News*.

'The first entry in the RAF Day Record Book for 29 Air Sea Rescue Unit, Littlehampton, on 13 August, 1943 is brief and to the point. It simply states that Duty Boat ST 442, Coxswain Bedford and crew, effected the pick-up of five Lancaster survivors, made a further search for two missing but nothing found: R.T.B. (returned to base), time and signature.

'This is a typical account kept by Air Sea Rescue Units in whatever field of operation. It often hides a story of heroism. While aircrew faced the dangers of enemy fighters, flak over enemy territory and long boring flights, the Air Sea Rescue services were to face equal hazards.

'The pick-up of ditched airmen was often at the risk of being within range of enemy guns, being chased by faster German E-boats, or attacked by enemy aircraft, and there was the danger of going to the aid of airmen unfortunate enough to have crashed in a minefield. The rescue crews carried out these tasks without question, but with a high degree of skill, in all types of weather.

'By nature, ASR men are a modest breed and perhaps that is why only two were ever to be awarded the George Medal in that service's short life by the time it disbanded in 1986.

'By the end of the Second World War more than 14,500 aircrew and others who went down in the sea were to owe their lives to this band of gallant men in wooden boats who made sure that "the sea did not have them".'

Bill Arden, now retired and living in Hamble on Southampton Water, had learned that a group of former Air Sea Rescue men were restoring three of their classic boats. His interest was awakened.

Fifty years ago Bill had reason to say 'thank you' to the crew of an Air Sea Rescue boat. How he was reintroduced to the very boat which picked him up is unique.

The selection of aircrew to fly as a group was often left to the particular pilot to sort out. Meeting in pubs, Flying Training Units, etc, small huddled groups were whispering. Soon men from all walks of civilian life were put together in a well-disciplined team.

Such a team had been picked by Flying Officer Bill Arden by the time they had completed training and had arrived at Woodhall Spa to join 619 Squadron, flying Lancasters, in 1943.

Dick Jones was navigator, 'Shep' Shepherd flight engineer, Ron Perkins bomb aimer, Vic Howarth wireless operator, Al Finch mid-upper gunner and Len Maddleford rear gunner. When 12 August arrived they had four trips to their credit; all seemed to be going well. The targets were in Germany; they had seen the odd German night fighter skidding by and the mighty fires of destruction below. Luck, never spoken about, appeared to be on their side.

12 August, 1943, was overcast. Briefing was called for at 1500 hours. Entering the large hall, Bill Arden noted from the number of crews in attendance that it was going to be a large raid. The Met Officer told them they could expect thick cloud for most of the trip but that the target area was clear. The cloud, both out and back, would serve as a haven from the German night fighters.

When the target map covering was removed by the briefing officer, the crews could see that the target that night was to be the Fiat works in Turin. It was to be a long haul: flying time there and back would be eight-and-a-half hours. The return would be quicker as the Lancasters would be lighter with the bombs gone and half the fuel used up. The stream would take off at 9.30 p.m. as dusk was setting in.

At the predicted time Bill's Lancaster was over the target, which was clear of thick cloud, and the bombs were dropped. They continued on the same flight path for a few more minutes to ensure they did not collide with other aircraft. Some flak was seen in the distance, but did not affect them. 'Shep' gave Bill a course for home and they sought the cover and safety of cloud for the return journey, out of sight of any roaming enemy fighters.

By 0430 it was still cloudy and quite dark. They should now be approaching landfall, so Bill began the slow descent for a visual. When they broke cloud, they were still out to sea and approaching the Isle of Wight. The cloud was patchy and lower, and the white horses they could see below in the gloom indicated a rough sea. Since the aircraft was flying perfectly well the tense atmosphere slowly started to evaporate. In forty minutes they would be home at Woodhall Spa enjoying a fried breakfast.

By this time they were over Selsey Bill in Sussex, a turning point for other bomber streams returning from raids on Europe. Without warning there was a big bang and the whole aircraft shook. After a stunned silence, a cry from Bill Arden told the crew that in the thick cloud they had hit another Lancaster, its image shrouded like a ghost for just a split second before impact, and then lost from view.

Damage in Bill's Lancaster was serious: a great chunk of the port wing buckled and fell away, and the port and starboard outer engines caught fire. Wireless operator Vic Howarth was by now calling 'May Day'. His calls for help were picked up at RAF Ford, near Arundel, a major diversion airfield. That night twenty-four heavy bombers were to land, either damaged or low on fuel and unable to return to their home bases. The Air Traffic Control asked whether Bill's aircraft could reach the airfield.

The stricken Lancaster, losing height, was hard to control and Bill Arden struggled to hold her steady. He told the crew to stand by for ditching stations and advised RAF Ford that his Lancaster was about to hit the sea some three miles south of Clymping.

The impact was severe. The Lancaster broke in half just behind the mid-upper gun turret position and Bill Arden was thrown against the instrument panel, gashing his head. He remembered nothing from then until his rescue, but the crew survivors were to tell him afterwards that he swam the fifty yards to the seven-man dinghy and was dragged in by the others.

Wet and cold, the survivors in the dinghy silently watched the nose of the Lancaster resurface, as if in defiance of its certain fate.

Shep Shepherd, the flight engineer, noticed that two members of their crew were missing; they could be afloat nearby – the Mae West was a good aircrew-saver.

Some 30 minutes later an RAF Walrus amphibian aircraft arrived. It had been scrambled from RAF Shoreham, along the coast from Brighton. Two attempts at landing were made but aborted because of the conditions, and the Walrus departed. A short time later two Spitfires flew over from RAF Merston, near Chichester, and dropped smoke marker flares to indicate the position. Just then an RAF Air Sea Rescue launch hove into view, a welcome sight on a cold, wet 13 August at 5.30 in the morning.

The Lancaster that had collided with Bill's aircraft had been low on fuel and was trying to land at Ford. The 207 Squadron aircraft was later to crash-land at Plaistow near Guildford, where all the NCO crew of Sergeants Cartwright, Crawford, Harman, Broadbent, Davidson, Goodson and Venton walked away without injury.

The rescue
The small Air Sea Rescue unit at Littlehampton was under the control of RAF Ford. ASR Unit 29 consisted of several rescue launches which were constantly switched with craft from other units, but in the main there were three boats on station. HSL 130 was a British-built 'Whaleback' powerboat with a creditable list of rescues, and there were two British powerboat seaplane tenders, ST 442 and 443. The small unit comprised two Flight Sergeants and fifteen airmen, the latter being either motorboat crews, wireless operators or engine fitters. Their base HQ was a shed near Littlehampton Golf Club. It was a tight and very efficient unit and during D-Day was in front-line action for many rescues. The shallow waters around Littlehampton were best suited to the seaplane tenders, which had a much shallower draught than the Whalebacks.

The standby crew on the night of 12/13 August, 1943, was under the command of F/Sgt Bedford and the duty boat was ST 442, powered by twin Perkins diesel engines which gave her a good turn of speed. The flight path to Ford airfield was directly overhead the ASR base, and that night had been busy. The boat crews were surprised that they had not been called out, but that was to change.

The May Day call had been sent to the Unit from Ford and ST 442 put to sea at 05.25. Clearing the harbour entrance, they headed for the last sighting made by the Spitfires which had dropped the marker flares. A mile farther on, Bill Arden and his crew were spotted and hauled aboard the rescue launch.

In spite of the conditions, ST 442 carried out a square search for several hours for the two missing crewmen, but without success. The survivors from the Lancaster were put ashore at Littlehampton jetty and taken to RAF Ford for medical attention before returning to their unit at Woodhall Spa.

The body of Len Maddleford was found the following day and that of Dick Jones three days later.

That was the last time Bill Arden was to fly with the survivors of his crew. While recovering in hospital he had his tonsils removed and teamed up with another crew before resuming operations on 27 September.

LUCKY OLD STAN

An American from Boston must be one of the most fortunate men to have survived the Second World War. Stan Rosoff was a navigator on a B.17 bomber of 340 Squadron, 97th Bomb Group USAAF, flying from a base in Italy early in 1944.

Stan already had thirty-five operational missions to his credit by 11 March, when his crew took off to bomb marshalling yards at Padua in Northern Italy. As usual the group of B.17s were flying in formation at a height of 22,000 feet.

By midday Stan's crew had reached Padua and successfully bombed their target. As the B.17 turned to set course back to base it was attacked by several Messerschmitt 109s; the enemy fighters scored several direct hits on Stan's aircraft, which was soon engulfed in fire.

Both the pilot and co-pilot were killed during the first attack. Three members only of the bomber's crew, including Stan Rosoff, were able to bale out. The bombardier only did so with the help of Stan's boot, which pushed him into the open bomb bay.

All three landed in the Gulf of Venice. As his parachute opened, Stan watched aghast as the B.17 exploded in midair and signalled the death of his three colleagues left on board.

Before they reached the sea, the three survivors had the terrifying experience of hanging helplessly beneath their parachutes as they were machine-gunned by one of the enemy fighters. Another of the survivors was killed as a result of this attack, either directly by the enemy's fire or by drowning in the Gulf.

After Stan hit the water he remembers retaining consciousness for a couple of minutes or so, owing to the extremely cold water, before he passed out. He came round six hours later in the home of an Italian fisherman. The boat had seen the parachutes coming down and had picked up the two survivors from the water.

Stan was sent to Venice to spend a few days in a German hospital to recover from the effects of the extreme cold he had suffered in the water. From there he was taken to the main interrogation centre for captured aircrew, near Frankfurt, where he was put into solitary confinement and interrogated, before receiving his first Red Cross parcel as a prisoner-of-war.

He was still at Dulag Luft on 23 March when the RAF raided Frankfurt, causing extensive damage and knocking out all utilities.

So, having survived the enemy fighter attack on the B.17, baled out just before the aircraft exploded, been machine-gunned as he hung under his parachute, lost consciousness in the freezing waters of the Gulf of Venice, experienced the terror of being underneath a major RAF bombing operation – Stan thinks he is a *very* lucky guy!

THE GIRL WHO DID A BLERIOT

The fact that these stories have so far concerned aircrew who were flying in the Second World War should not lead to the assumption that the act of ditching was entirely a male preserve. The following account involves a young and quite glamorous lady who qualified for membership of the Goldfish Club and, in fact, made a considerable hit with the elderly members when she attended the Club's Annual Dinner at Stratford-on-Avon a few years ago.

Gloria Pullan was piloting a Bleriot type XI monoplane, circa 1909 (yes, you have got to believe it) when she ditched within sight of the famous White Cliffs of Dover on 26 July, 1989.

The story began just eighty years earlier when Louis Bleriot became the first man to cross the English Channel in an aeroplane. In 1989 his grandson, also named Louis, determined to mark the eightieth anniversary with a re-run of that historic flight, using an exactly similar machine.

Like the original crossing, it was bound to be a rather touch-and-go venture and, as weight had to be kept to the absolute minimum, Monsieur Bleriot junior turned to Gloria to do the job.

After the aircraft and the 25 horsepower Anzani engine had been fully overhauled, a number of test flights were carried out at Old Warden. It is reported that the combination of a grass runway and an undercarriage dependent in the main on 'bungee' rubber cord led Gloria to comment, 'I shall need to wear a tighter bra!'

With such attention to detail are the best flight plans made. At 05.00 on the appointed day she took off from Marck airfield, near Calais, closely followed by escort aircraft. Initially, all went well and the Bleriot type XI climbed steadily at 45 m.p.h. to a height of about 1,300 feet.

Suddenly there was a severe loss of power as the engine overheated. The plane lost height slowly, coming within sight of Dover. Eventually, however, what Gloria described as 'an extremely gentle belly-flop' was made just two and a half miles off the English coast.

She was picked up by an RAF Air Sea Rescue helicopter within a few minutes. The aircraft was upended by rotor wash but remained afloat owing to the installation of a polystyrene brick and was duly recovered.

'We missed by a whisker,' said Gloria, 'but I'll be ready and waiting next time.' The aircraft was put on display in Selfridge's store in Oxford Street, London, the following day, just as its predecessor had been in 1909.

'SHEILAS!' – AND THEN THERE WERE NONE

It is time to disillusion any of our readers who may have thought that the joint compilers of this anthology have had only second-hand experience of ditching, gained from the various stories they have assembled. Not so: they both got their feet wet more than fifty years ago.

Jim Burtt-Smith and John French were pilot and wireless operator respectively on a Mark III Wellington of 115 Squadron, operating from Marham in Norfolk in 1942. Lionel Harcus, the bomb-aimer, hailed from Essex, while the navigator, Barney D'ath-Weston and the rear gunner, Bill Frizzell, were New Zealanders.

The crew had first come together at No.11 Operational Training Unit at Bassingbourn, near Royston in Hertfordshire in 1941. They soon began to work well together and enjoyed the many long-distance training flights over the length and breadth of Britain which formed part of their preparation for bombing missions over Germany.

At the beginning these trips were invariably made in daylight hours and only in favourable weather. One of their favourite excursions took them across England from east to west as far as Aberystwyth on the Welsh coast. It lasted about five hours.

On reaching the Welsh coast it was Jim's habit to bring the aircraft down to a height of about fifty feet, open the throttles as wide as possible and roar across the Irish Sea before bringing the Wellington up into a steep climb and turning back on a course to base. He said it relieved the frustration of flying straight and level for a few hours. On these 'beat-ups' John was occasionally in the front turret firing into the sea with the twin Brownings. He found the low flying over the wavetops (at that time) quite exhilarating.

103

At least it was more fun than sitting hunched over the radio set, taking loop bearings from the various direction-finding transmitters scattered throughout the country.

On one exercise the Wellington was skimming over the edge of the beach when a shout from Barney came over the inter-com, 'Sheilas!' This word may be unfamiliar to those without contact with our Antipodean cousins, but it can be translated in English as 'Women!' or in American as 'Dames!' Looking out of the aircraft, Barney had spotted some young female bodies lying on the beach in the sun. With the exception of Jim, and Bill Frizzell in the rear turret, we jumped up to see the sights.

A moment before John had been taking some bearings on the radio. Signals were received on the 'trailing aerial' – a length of woven wire with a number of lead weights on the end, which had to be wound out from a reel so that it extended beneath the aircraft. It was about sixty feet long overall.

As the aircraft sped along the beach the crew could see the girls quite clearly; they were waving. The Wellington then went into a steep, climbing turn as Jim pulled the control column back and headed out towards sea.

At the end of the beach was a jetty, and at the end of the jetty was a statue. The crew often speculated about who it represented; perhaps it was Lloyd George. They could not think of any other famous Welshman justifying such a monument.

As the Wellington climbed higher and passed the end of the jetty there was a sharp crack, audible above the engine noise, and a jerk in the fuselage similar to the effect upon a car when the brakes are applied suddenly. John was still looking back at the beach. The statue came into view and he saw to his horror that his trailing aerial was winding itself furiously around the neck of the figure like a South American bola.

For a few days the crew were anxious that the Local Authority might have regarded the assault on the guardian of the bay as an insult to the Welsh nation and demand some manner of retribution through the Air Ministry. Fortunately nothing more was heard, but the loss of his trailing aerial cost John the sum of five shillings, and in those days five bob bought several pints of beer.

Having progressed to night cross-country trips, the crew finally concluded their operational training and at the end of June, 1942, after fourteen days' leave, they reported to 115 Squadron at Marham for the serious business of making some large holes in Germany. The first two operational missions in early July were to Bremen and Wilhelmshaven and were the cause of some excitement to the crew. Fear had not yet developed and the sights they saw beneath them over enemy territory were unique: lights of all colours darting through and exploding into the blackness like fireworks on a cosmic scale and patches of brilliant scarlet dotted over the backcloth where the incendiary bombs had created havoc in the towns below. Only later did the novelty fade, replaced by the burgeoning realization that those pretty coloured lights were potentially deadly and if their nativity occurred too close to a Wellington bomber the crew's fascination would be abruptly ended, with no more time for applause.

The crew completed two 'gardening' trips successfully off the Dutch coast and were then briefed to return to Germany and wreak havoc on the industrial town of Duisburg in the Ruhr. In advance of this operation, however, there was some atonement to be made for a *faux pas* which had occurred on the return to base from the second minelaying trip. Coming in to land, Jim had for some reason overshot the runway and when the Wellington at last came to rest it was enveloped in barbed wire. This encircled the airfield on the outer perimeter and was presumably intended to prevent the incursion of stray sheep or cattle rather than to deter the progress of enemy agents. To this day that point on the outer rim of Marham aerodrome is known as 'Smith's Gap'. For his sins, Jim was instructed to spend part of the following night practising 'circuits and bumps'; and so, for an hour and a half, Crew Eleven (as they were known) suffered the boredom of circling the airfield repeatedly as Jim touched down, opened the throttles and took off again, touched down . . . and so ad infinitum. The rest of the crew agreed that it was more fun over Germany.

The operation to Duisburg came and went without incident. During the ensuing gap of several days when no operational flying occurred, the crew began to speculate where their next target might be. The day arrived for briefing – and the target? Duisburg. Again the trip was uneventful and Crew Eleven heaved a collective sigh of relief as the welcoming flarepath at Marham flashed by beneath the Wellington's wheels.

Two nights later the members of Crew Eleven reported for briefing once again. As the map cover was drawn aside and the briefing officer approached with his pointer, a collective groan arose from the assembled bomber crews and was punctuated by some unrepeatable expressions of disgust and disbelief. Someone shouted, 'Who the hell have they got in Duisburg – Hitler?'

For Jim and his colleagues this operation proved to be their 'baptism of fire'. As they flew over the city, straight and level, with Lionel's thumb on the bomb-release button, all was quiet. Maybe the flak crews in 'Happy Valley' (the Ruhr) were having a night off. The illusion was soon shattered. The interior of the Wellington, without any warning, was suddenly ablaze with light as the aircraft was pinpointed by a blue master searchlight: its aim had been as precise as that of a professional sniper. Seconds later the Wellington was engulfed in a cone of searchlights which homed in on the master.

Jim shouted, 'Hold on, lads!' as he went into a steep, spiralling dive, the only recognized method of escaping from an enemy searchlight cone. The sky around them was now speckled with exploding flak and the noise of the engines rose to a crescendo like the scream of a cornered beast. After what the crew felt to be an hour but was in fact less than half a minute, darkness fell once more inside the aircraft. More than eight thousand feet had been lost in the manoeuvre, but at least the Wellington was now on course for the North Sea and the safety of the English coast.

There followed the luxury of one night off, spent by some of the crew with many others from 115 Squadron in exploring the pubs of King's Lynn. How quickly could the war be forgotten! Playing darts, chatting up local girls or barmaids, singing familiar choruses while the beer flowed freely, such simple pleasures were remarkably effective therapy for dissipating tension and relaxing body and mind. Effective but ephemeral. By the following afternoon, as yet another operation was announced, the stomach knots and headaches would return and there was no escape.

None of Crew Eleven welcomed the prospect of yet another trip to Duisburg. 'Leave it to me,' said Jim. 'I've got an idea. We're certainly not going to let those Jerries do what they did last time.' Later he turned to Lionel. 'I want you to tell me the moment you see the Rhine coming up. Then get ready to drop the bombs.' The others began to wonder what their pilot was up to.

That night there was broken cloud cover and the Wellington met with no opposition as it approached the target. Lionel was already lying on the floor of the aircraft looking through the lower escape hatch when he shouted, 'The river's in sight, Skip! Dead ahead – about a mile.'

The note of the engines rose slightly as Jim opened the throttles. The faint gleam of the water was now visible below. The aircraft was approaching the west bank of the Rhine, with Duisburg opposite on the east bank. Jim shouted, 'Stand by to release bombs when I tell you!' This was most unusual. Lionel would normally instruct the pilot to fly straight and level until the target was in the bomb-sight.

The river was now beneath the aircraft. The engines roared as the throttles were opened wide and the Wellington banked steeply to the left. 'Drop the bombs – now!' Jim shouted. Back came the reply, 'Bombs gone!' By the time they hit the ground Crew Eleven's Wellington had turned through 180 degrees and was scooting back towards the Dutch coast. The overall flying time on that night was nearly half an hour less than on the previous excursions to Duisburg. We learned later that night fighters had been waiting over the Ruhr and thirty-six of our bombers had been lost.

Being neither a physicist nor a mathematician, Jim had devised his plan for bombing Duisburg without crossing the river on the simple principle of the sling-shot. He considered that if the bombs left an aircraft flying at an angle of 45 degrees to the ground while travelling in a half-circle at about 250 miles an hour, they should fall in an arc and reach the ground at a point not far away from where they would have landed had they been dropped vertically. We shall never know. What is certain, however, is that Crew Eleven had had their fill of the Duisburg illuminations.

Had they had foreknowledge of subsequent events, Jim and his colleagues might possibly have agreed to complete the remainder of their operational tour – at that time thirty trips – flying a shuttle service to Duisburg. But the future was unknown and a bomber crew had no option but to go where they were sent. It was considered by some that High Command picked out their targets with a pin. Others felt that the 'brass hats' regarded operational missions simply as an extension of training: 'Let's give the boys some long-distance practice tomorrow and see if the fuel lasts out. Jolly good idea!'

However such crucial decisions were made, the target chosen by the RAF National Lottery for the night of 26 July, 1942, was Hamburg. As a main base for the German navy, and particularly the U-boat fleet, it was surpassed only by Berlin in the strength of defence against attack from the air.

Two days earlier Crew Eleven had taken delivery of a new Wellington. Previously, all their operations had been flown in aircraft vacated by other crews who, by reason of sickness or decimation, could not participate on the night in question. The brand new aircraft was to be their very own; it circled the airfield and they saw it make a perfect landing and taxi towards the hangars. It came to a halt and out stepped a small but attractive young lady in the uniform of the Air Transport Auxiliary. She was Joan Hughes, later to become an instructor to budding post-war pilots of British European Airways. In order to fly the Wellington she had to resort to a pair of wooden blocks carried in her equipment. These were clipped on to the rudder bars to compensate for her lack of leg-length. They were shapely, well-proportioned – but short. (No, *not* the blocks).

The aircraft was B for Bertie. Jim and his crew took it up for the customary air test and it behaved admirably. Before take-off the crew were joined by a Wing Commander who was clearly impressed by Joan Hughes' achievement. He remarked to Crew Eleven, 'A little girl like that brought that plane in with no trouble, while you big oafs can't even land properly!' He must have been familiar with Smith's Gap.

On the night of 26 July B for Bertie took off for Hamburg with a full load of incendiaries. This was in pre-Pathfinder days: they were to be one of the first aircraft over the target and their incendiaries would mark the aiming point for the main force.

In spite of moderate flak over Hamburg, the target was bombed without incident and Jim turned the aircraft, heading for the nearest cloud cover. Somewhere near Wilhelmshaven Jim had just accepted a beaker of coffee from John when he saw the flash of an explosion as the port engine was hit and clouds of smoke billowed out. Jim pressed the extinguisher button for that side and as the fire died out he de-feathered the engine and opened the throttle on the starboard engine, but it refused to respond beyond 1,800 revs – not enough to maintain height. What followed was best described by Jim himself in his book *One of the Many on the Move*:

'We threw out everything that wasn't bolted down. I tried to start the port engine, but no joy. I dived: still no joy, and I lost valuable height doing so. When you consider it was a new plane, it should have been easy to maintain height and even to climb on one engine: but no – the toggle-switch was u/s and I could not get back into manual control.

'The day before, on the air test, I had flown first on one engine and then on the other. What had gone wrong? Long after, I found out that most of the ancillary equipment – dynamos and motor – worked off the port engine. When that went for a Burton, so did a lot of our equipment including the working of the automatic pitch control.

'We were down to about 12,000 feet and gradually losing height. I called Lionel out of the front turret to hang on to the right rudder bar to stop the aircraft veering to port. I applied full rudder bias and with our combined efforts we managed to head seawards, though the plane still wanted to pull to the left. I was flying right wing down to help to counteract the drag. We staggered on, with the flak still following us, hoping against hope that there were no German fighters about. There was plenty of encouragement from the crew, but I had to tell them that I didn't think I could make it home and that they had two choices: jump or ditch! 'We'll take our chances with you,' they all agreed.

' "I'll try to make base. If not, it's the drink." Carried unanimously. We threw out everything that was loose, including the Elsan toilet, flares, etc, but *not* the emergency rations. I was still struggling with the controls, and Lionel had been relieved by John. I wanted Lionel in the front turret in case any marauding night fighters turned up.

'I am writing this so calmly now, but at the time it was bloody hairy. Anyone who was on operations and says he was never scared must be lying. I don't mind telling you, I was scared stiff. We were now down to 6,000 feet and the starboard engine was playing up. Try as I might, I could not maintain height. We were still making some progress towards the coast and were still flying in cloud, thank God. We could still see the reflections of the fires of Hamburg. Then Frizzo piped up, "Just saw a plane slide past in the mist. Couldn't see whether it was friend or foe." It would not have made much difference if it had hit us!

'With this thought in mind, I let B for Bertie sink slowly through the cloud, dropping to 4,000 feet as we came out. All this time John had been busy sending out an SOS, while Barney destroyed the secret papers. I knew we would never make base. We were now losing height fast and I told Barney to give me a new course for home. The ack-ack was still pounding away. As we flew lower and lower we came withing range of the light ack-ack; shrapnel was whizzing through the aircraft and we were taking a pounding.

'As we headed for the open sea I called the boys on the inter-com and told them we would have to ditch, but that I would try to get as far out to sea as possible. As we left the Dutch coast behind us, Frizzo called out that the searchlights were pointing out our course for the fighters. We were still losing height and all the instruments were on the blink. Outside it was as black as the Ace of Spades.

'I shouted to John to let the trailing aerial down and clamp the Morse key. I knew that when the aerial touched the sea I would have about 60 feet to spare. That was the only way I could judge our height. In spite of all our efforts it was still impossible to steer a straight course. I estimated that by this time we were about 90 miles out from Holland and I gave instructions to take up ditching positions. It was still as black as a November fog.

'As John and Lionel left the flight deck, opening the escape hatch above my head, I jettisoned the remaining fuel, shut off the starboard engine and headed (as I thought) for England. By this time the plane was wallowing like a sick cow. I had to keep playing with the stick to keep her airborne, letting the nose go down, then pulling up a little – just like a glider. I was praying for a moon. If I couldn't see the waves to judge which way to land, we would plunge straight in and down. It was essential to land towards the waves with the tail down; any other way was disastrous.

'John shouted out, "Sixty feet!" and I told the lads to hold tight – we were going in. Frizzo turned his turret to starboard so that he could get out when we crashed. There we were, plunging down –

to what? This is it, I thought: there was no way we could survive in the inky blackness. Once more I prayed for just enough light to allow me to land the right way. And then the moon came out! At almost zero feet I managed to turn, with the moon shining on the sea and acting as a flare-path. I literally flew down the moonbeams. Hold tight – nose up. There was one almighty crash and then silence. The moon promptly disappeared.

'I was under water, but my Mae West brought me to the surface. One by one we scrambled out on to the wing. The dinghy popped out of the nacelle hatch and started to inflate; Frizzo clambered along the fuselage, while John and Barney had climbed through the astrodome carrying with them our survival kit.

'We scrambled quickly into the dinghy. The Wellington floated for about thirty seconds and Lionel cut the cord without delay, otherwise we would have been dragged down with her. In fact the dinghy was still not fully inflated as the plane sank slowly beneath the waves, leaving five frightened but thankful men bobbing about on a piece of rubber measuring about 6 feet in diameter. The time was approximately 1 a.m. This, then, was our apprenticeship to membership of the most exclusive club in the world – the Goldfish Club.

'We took stock of our situation. It was dark; the raid was still in progress with our bombers still heading for the target. We could see the twin red exhausts as one flew overhead. John sent out an SOS by torch and – wonder of wonders – received the colours of the day in return. We threw the drogue overboard to stop the dinghy from spinning, and a couple of fluorescent tablets. We all did some bailing out, but our feet were saturated. Someone handed cigarettes out and even the non-smokers had a puff: anything to calm the nerves. To hope that five men would ever be picked up from the middle of the North Sea – a small speck in the ocean – seemed highly improbable.

'I said a prayer that we would be picked up by someone. It was getting lighter by the minute and a suggestion was made by one of the crew that we should open up the rations. (It must have been Lionel!) I did not agree; there was no telling how long we would be in the water.

'The mist was thinning but it remained very cold indeed and I didn't relish the thought of lasting out for days on end. Then

111

suddenly we heard the unmistakable sound of a plane and spotted it far in the distance. It looked like a JU 88. We crouched down in the dinghy to make as small a target as possible, since we had heard how some enemy aircraft had fired on dinghies and parachutes. Apparently he had not seen us and we resumed paddling steadily northwards. We could not send out any distress calls as there was no portable radio. Our dinghy was an early type, with no canopy – just a round circle of rubber, like a tractor's inner tube, but it kept us afloat.

'Somewhere around ten o'clock we heard another plane. "There she is!" shouted Frizzo and pointed east. Straining our eyes we could just make out the distant silhouette of a multi-engined plane. We all agreed that it must be one of ours, probably a Sunderland. I grabbed the marine distress signal, pulled off the adhesive strip and threw it into the water. The flare, held aloft, gaily sent out coloured balls at intervals: then out of the mist loomed a three-engined seaplane, heading straight towards us with the front turret swinging round menacingly.

'Of course it was German (there is still some controversy about its make) and it landed some way off, slowly taxied towards our dinghy with the front guns trained on us and finally pulled up alongside.

'Barney threw the rations overboard – where they were easily retrieved by the German crew as they were conveniently stored in a waterproof case. "Should have eaten the bloody stuff!" muttered Lionel. To think of all that lovely chocolate filling German bellies was ironic, to say the least.

'They helped us on board and I was taken to the captain, who uttered the famous last words, "For you, my friend, the war is over". I think that must have been included in their training. He gave me a cigarette and asked what our target had been. I said, "If you came out searching for us you already know what our target was." It turned out that he had been a pilot with Lufthansa before the war and knew England quite well.

'We took off as I stood beside him, with the rest of our crew scattered about the aircraft. There was a strong smell of diesel everywhere and the noise was deafening. As the metal body took the brunt of the waves the plane was a long time becoming airborne. When we eventually lifted off the rear gunner fired a short burst and sank our dinghy.

'It did cross my mind that we might have had a go at capturing the plane, but without any weapons and suffering from exposure we would not have had much chance, so we resigned ourselves to the inevitable. I must say that the German crew treated us well on the return trip to their base.'

The seaplane landed in the harbour at Nordeney, one of the most northerly of the Frisian islands. Jim and his companions were put into separate cells and given their first meal in captivity, consisting of an unidentifiable soup with meat balls, followed by boiled, sliced cucumber with sugar as dessert, and a cup of 'ersatz' coffee (made from acorns). Egon Ronay would not have been impressed.

In typical German fashion, each man's possessions were taken away, examined and recorded. Any Air Ministry items were confiscated, but the remaining personal belongings were returned to the owner with a typewritten list in German. One of the crew, who shall be nameless, had carried a condom in his wallet: failing to understand the German translation on the list he pointed it out to the guard. 'Was ist?' The guard almost collapsed in helpless laughter before demonstrating with finger and thumb of one hand and forefinger of the other the precise function of the mystery item.

In their three years of captivity, no member of Crew Eleven discovered whether any alternative use had been found within the confines of the prison camp for that unusual import.

GETTING ABOARD THE M.T.B.
WAS THE WORST

On 21 June, 1944, the crew of Lancaster A-Able of 57 Squadron were among those detailed to attack a synthetic oil plant at Wesseling, fifteen miles south of Cologne.

It was a fine, clear night as they left their base at East Kirkby in Lincolnshire and began the long climb with their bomb load, comprising a 4,000 lb 'Cookie' blast bomb and sixteen 500 lb high explosive bombs. They had been told at briefing that crews of the USAAF 'heavies' operating over Germany earlier that day had reported attacks by black-painted night fighters, so it was assumed that fighter opposition would be reduced.

As Flight Engineer, Geoff Copeman had a good view forward and as the Lancaster neared the Dutch coast he could see the flak ahead. Twenty miles farther on it ceased, to be replaced by fighter flares. Soon aircraft were falling in flames to left and right. Mysterious lights were seen darting across the sky and the crew could only conjecture that they might be the rockets regularly faced by the USAAF.

Eventually the aircraft turned on to an easterly course to take them between Aachen and Düsseldorf, heading directly for Cologne. This was a deliberately misleading manoeuvre, however; fifteen miles from the city the Lancaster turned towards the oil plant.

The night fighters had returned to base to refuel and re-arm, but the flak was very heavy. A-Able weaved slightly while the crew awaited instructions. There was cloud over the target and only ten minutes from 'H-hour' this forced a change in the marking plan. Eventually the bomber turned into the attack together with the other silhouettes. For an eternity the skipper held the controls steady until the Lancaster leapt upwards as the bombs dropped off to the bomb-aimer's shout of 'Bombs away!' They made a slowly descending turn to the right and levelled out on a homeward course, well below any stragglers still heading for the target.

They had hardly settled on course when the mid-upper gunner, John Johnson, called a warning. As the pilot instinctively pushed the Lancaster's nose down the crew were dazzled by a yellow glare as a rocket streaked by over the aircraft, which rocked violently as another exploded below. Crossing the Belgian border, the plane made another sudden dive, this time quite an involuntary one, and Geoff Copeman remembers being lifted from the floor. The rear gunner later recalled seeing a puff of smoke below the starboard wing, but he had disregarded it at the time.

They were dead on track and as they reached the coast all seemed well. Suddenly, however, the aircraft's nose dipped yet again, this time with much more violence and Geoff was thrown across the fuselage. As he got to his feet he found that both starboard engines had cut. He checked the gauges on his panel and saw that the tanks in use were empty: about two hundred gallons of fuel were unaccounted for. Before he could change tanks another engine died and the fourth misfired. The gauges for the main tanks indicated that six hundred gallons remained, as expected, and he quickly switched over the feed lines. All engines fired again, but before the pilot could turn on to a direct course for the English coast the glow of the exhausts died once more. Only the port outer engine ran on, spluttering, despite every change of feed lines. An unladen Lancaster would climb on three engines and maintain height on two, but in this situation there was no choice: Geoff feathered the three engines just as he heard the captain's order, 'Dinghy, dinghy! Prepare for ditching!'

To improve buoyancy Geoff jettisoned the remaining fuel and carried out the rest of his ditching drill. As he went back to the rest bed, his crash position, Fred the wireless operator was leaving his set after having transmitted the aircraft's position as a 'fix'. The crew never discovered whether his Mayday signals were picked up by anyone.

Plugged into the inter-com, Geoff was in touch with his skipper as he warned the crew of decreasing height. At two hundred feet Geoff pulled off his helmet and shouted, 'Brace for impact!' The Lancaster hit the sea with a crash which flung Geoff upwards and slammed him against the roof of the fuselage. There followed a rending screech, accompanied by the hissing of air and oxygen from broken pipes as the rear of the fuselage was torn off. Then the Lancaster bounced. The second impact was surprisingly light. Geoff jumped up quickly and stuck his head out of the hatch above. A wave broke over him and he found himself spitting out a vile mixture of oil, salt water and blood from his split nose. He carried an axe to release the dinghy, but it was not needed; as he dropped down on to the wing he met John Johnson arriving from the rear hatch. The dinghy inflated quickly; just as everyone climbed aboard the wing became awash and the dinghy floated over the leading edge. As the Lancaster filled with water it became very nose-heavy and the wing threatened to overturn on to the dinghy. Plunging their arms into the water, the crew paddled furiously towards the wing-tip and drifted clear as A-Able sank to her resting place. It had been her fortieth operation.

It was about 2.20 in the morning and fairly dark. A heavy swell was running, with white horses on the wave tops. A small slit in the bottom of the dinghy was soon plugged, though not before the crew's legs and feet were soaked. The pilot had been badly cut about the face as a result of his head having gone through the Perspex above him, and the navigator had sustained a crack on the head.

Having raised the weather-sheet around the dinghy, the crew huddled beneath it to wait for daylight, seeking what small comfort there was between bouts of sea-sickness. Dawn broke at about four-thirty, by which time the dinghy had drifted clear of the oily slick on the water. The sea-sickness eased, although Nick the pilot was rather weak. The bomb-aimer spent some time patching his cuts, while the rest of the crew erected the aerial mast. It was fear-fully cold and this was a warming exercise, as also was the baling out which had to be continued while endless waves washed over the dinghy, bringing with them the green stain of the fluorescent sea marker which was trailing over the side.

The radio was assembled – but there was a problem: Bill, the navigator, had collected the pack containing the rockets and kite-aerial from the aircraft, but in his dazed state at the moment of ditching he had merely passed them over the side. They still had the mast, but the range of transmission was considerably reduced and after a short time the bakelite joint at the bottom broke. Geoff and another colleague tried to hold the fracture together while the others pulled on the stays to keep the mast upright as the dinghy rose and fell with the waves. In the end the flexibility of the dinghy beat them and, to make matters worse, the hand-operated crank mechanism which powered the radio could hardly be turned. The grease had become stiff in the freezing conditions.

At about six o'clock a USAAF Thunderbolt fighter passed about half a mile away, but the pilot apparently had his mind on other matters. By eleven-thirty the clouds began to break up and the sun shone through. Fewer waves were washing into the dinghy and some steady baling reduced the water level to a mere inch or two. The crew began to feel a little more comfortable.

Nick, who had been lying very quiet, suddenly raised himself and said he could hear a plane. The rest of the crew listened, but heard nothing. Nick was quite positive: he thought it sounded like a Wellington. A few minutes later, sure enough, a 'Wimpey' appeared on the horizon to the north and then two more were seen. All three turned away, reappearing in the east; the crew in the dinghy could tell that a 'square search' was being made. At last one turned and flew low over the dinghy; it circled for nearly an hour, before flashing a signal, 'Help coming'. Then it disappeared over the horizon.

Things began to look quite promising when a pair of Air Sea Rescue Hudson aircraft arrived on the scene, but an hour later a 'Lindholme' dinghy was dropped nearby. This large, boat-shaped inflatable had supply containers attached. The crew's first reaction was the depressing thought that they were to spend another night afloat. And their depression was compounded by the fact the tow line was found to be broken and they could only watch helplessly as the Lindholme drifted by out of reach. The only consolation was that the Hudson crew would probably have seen what happened.

By three-thirty that afternoon the crew of A-Able were alone once more. Shortly before five, however, something caught Geoff's eye as the dinghy rose on the waves. As it lifted again, he could see a mast. Within minutes, what looked like a battleship was wallowing some yards away. As a sailor prepared to throw a rope, Geoff stood up in the dinghy. The rope was thrown to – or at – Geoff. Wet and heavy, with a knot on the end, it caught him squarely on the ear. A net was lowered down the side of the boat and, as Geoff was nearest, he was the first to negotiate the apparently simple task of boarding. As the boat rolled to port, the lower edge reached the dinghy. Geoff waited for the right moment, took a firm grip and stepped on to the bottom rung of the net. The boat rolled back to starboard: Geoff took off and flew over the ship's rail. The rest of the crew followed, one after another, to be hurled aboard and spreadeagled on the deck.

Despite the violent arrival, Nick was now much recovered; he and Geoff were put into a little sick-bay and given dry clothes. Geoff was leaning over to examine his damaged nose in the mirror when the engines were opened up, the launch leapt forward and Geoff was thrown towards the washbasin, cutting his forehead on the water tank above. As a fresh trickle of blood oozed out, he suggested to Nick that it might be 'one of those days'. However, by the time they had shared one tumbler of Scotch and another of rum the world seemed a much happier place.

It took the vessel – a motor torpedo boat converted to rescue work – a couple of hours to reach Great Yarmouth, where those damaged members of the Lancaster's crew were taken to the naval hospital. Nick received twenty-six stitches. Geoff mentioned that his left knee was very sore, probably from the collision with the roof of the Lancaster. An X-ray revealed nothing, but the doctor was nevertheless very interested. 'I was looking for frostbite,' he said. 'In June?' Geoff said incredulously. The doctor nodded. 'Any month will do in the North Sea.'

Not until the following Saturday after returning to base did the crew learn of the toll exacted by the Wesseling raid on the force of 120 Lancasters. On the shortest and brightest night of the year, they had been sent to attack the most heavily defended area of Europe, sitting ducks for the FW 190 day fighters with their 120 mm rockets. No fewer than thirty-seven bombers had been lost – more than the total effort from East Kirkby. Of those crews, only the seven from A-Able and six from another aircraft returned home. Two hundred and forty-six airmen were missing. Sixty-four of them had sat down for tea with the crew of A-Able on that Wednesday afternoon.

Crew of A-Able:
Pilot: P.O. Edgar Nicklin (RNZAF)
Flt.Engr.:   Sgt. Geoff Copeman
Navigator: F.O. Bill Martin
Air Bomber: F/Sgt. Philip Baker (RNZAF)
W/Op: F/Sgt. Fred Foster
Mid-U Gunner: Sgt. John Johnson
Rear Gunner: Sgt. Jack Hobbs

ANOTHER RESCUE BY FRITZ

In 1943 Basil Williams from Auckland, Royal New Zealand Air Force, was the rear gunner on a Wellington flying with 432 Squadron of the Royal Canadian Air Force from Eastmoor in Yorkshire. On 22 September a total of 711 aircraft including Lancasters, Halifaxes, Stirlings and Wellingtons, together with five USAAF B.17 bombers, mounted the first major raid on the German city of Hanover for two years.

Basil reports that the flight to Hanover was reasonably quiet, but on reaching the target 'all hell broke loose'. The Wellington was coned by searchlights and came under heavy attack from German flak. The pilot, Sgt Len Tierney, put the plane into a steep dive, lost several thousand feet, and then pulled the Wellington up so abruptly that Basil felt his turret was in danger of breaking away from the aircraft and that his eardrums would burst. For several seconds he was suspended in midair, held only by his seat belt. According to Len Tierney, the speedometer needle hit the end of its register.

The Wellington regained height and the bombs were dropped. The pilot then asked the navigator, P.O. Dick Sewell to check the remaining fuel. His first reply was 'sixty gallons'; then a correction – 'nothing'. If the gauges were correct, the only fuel left was in the Wellington's nacelle tanks. How far would that carry them? Should they head for Sweden, bale out over enemy territory or set course for home across the North Sea? The last option was the favourite.

Sure enough, after they had crossed the Dutch coast the engines failed. Basil turned his turret at right angles in readiness for the ditching, but as the Wellington hit the water the force of impact turned the turret back by several degrees and Basil had a struggle to squeeze through the aperture. Standing on the tail plane in the blackness, he saw the white face of the wireless operator, Johnny Mercer, drifting by in the water. Basil shouted, 'Grab the tail plane!' Johnny said later that those few words probably saved his life.

While they had been on leave in Kilmarnock, home town of the bomb aimer, P.O. Les Whitton, he and Basil had bought small sheath knives. Having scrambled up from the tail plane on to the main fuselage, Basil slid along towards the front of the Wellington using his knife to give some purchase. The waves were now breaking over the doomed aircraft, which was sinking fast. Eventually Basil managed to join Les Whitton and Dick Sewell, who were standing on the wing. From out of the darkness they heard a whistle blown and saw the pilot close by the aircraft with the dinghy. Basil was first aboard, pulled in the navigator and then the wireless operator, who had a badly gashed forehead and was almost unconscious. At last all five members of the crew were safely in the dinghy.

A sheath knife lay on the rubber floor and was quickly thrown overboard, together with anything else with sharp points or edges. The dinghy had no leak stoppers – and no storm sheet. Exhausted and soaked to the skin, the five airmen soon drifted into unconsciousness.

Day followed night, and night followed day. The very limited supplies were carefully rationed: one mouthful of water, a few Horlicks tablets and one square of glucose or barley sugar per day. The nights, says Basil Williams, were the worst – there were dreams. One night he dreamed they had landed in South Africa and had been offered wine, which he refused. All he wanted was water.

Early on the fourth day a JU 88 flew over the dinghy, followed shortly after by a German flying boat, which dropped a flare to mark their position. Basil grudgingly felt that the bright red dye colouring the water around them was an improvement on the green chemical used by the RAF. Having believed in their youthful optimism that they had drifted towards the English coast, the crew were inspired by the sight of enemy aircraft to begin paddling again with all their remaining strength, but to no avail. A German air sea rescue boat finally arrived and, after throwing away their escape packs (complete with foreign currency), the Wellington's survivors were helped aboard. In the cabin they all undressed: quite a feat, said Basil, as all their sodden clothing had shrunk and their arms and legs were swollen. The Germans told them that the search had been going on for days. Some cognac was passed round and the atmosphere became quite amicable. One German crew member had worked for several years in London, while another had been in Glasgow. Eventually the boat docked at the island of Borkum in the Frisian Islands.

Interrogation began the next day. Basil was offered a cigarette and annoyed his interrogator by refusing. Les Whitton, who had some schoolboy French, was a particular target for German anger as he persistently refused to give more information than name, rank and number. At one point the threat was made to take him outside and shoot him.

After two or three nights at Borkum, the Wellington crew were taken to either Emden or Bremerhaven by ferry. On the way Basil succeeded in making two small German children laugh, but they were immediately dragged away from his 'evil influence' by their mother. Their subsequent train journey through the Ruhr, during which they were shouted at, spat at and threatened, ended at Frankfurt, whence they were transferred to the main interrogation centre for RAF prisoners. Dick Sewell and Les Whitton were sent to Stalag Luft III at Sagan (setting for the famous 'Wooden Horse' escape), while the other three crew members ended up in Lithuania. All returned home safely after the end of the war. The only casualty was Len Tierney, the pilot, who had suffered severe frostbite and had all his toes amputated at Grantham hospital.

A KIWI ROBINSON CRUSOE

To be adrift in a rubber dinghy in the North Sea was never a pleasant experience, as so many former Second World War aircrew have confirmed. But to ditch in the Pacific Ocean was something else.

In the North Sea or the English Channel, or even the eastern Atlantic, there was always the fairly confident hope of rescue: at best by the RAF Air Sea Rescue Service or the Royal Navy, or at worst by the Germans. To ditch in the vast expanses of the Pacific, however, brought no such encouragement to the luckless airmen. Unless their position was known and U.S. warships were in the vicinity, there was every possibility that they would drift ashore on to one of the myriad islands and be taken into custody, at best, by the Japanese occupying forces: not a happy prospect.

One of the few who did survive the hazards of a Pacific ditching was Flight Sergeant George Luoni, another New Zealander of the RNZAF, flying a P.40 Kittyhawk with 17 Fighter Squadron on 23 September, 1943. Eight Kittyhawks were providing top cover at 11,000 feet for American bombers carrying out a raid on AA positions near Kahili in the Solomon Islands. Over the target the fighters were jumped by about ten Japanese Zeros. One attacked George Luoni's Kittyhawk and hit the oil tank and cowling in several places. Oil spurted into the cockpit and over the canopy.

Losing height slowly, George broke formation and headed for the Treasury Islands, where the Intelligence Officer had declared the natives to be very friendly. As the oil pressure fell to zero the engine began running very roughly and smoke filled the cockpit. George realized he had only one option: he rolled the aircraft on to its back and baled out at 4,000 feet. Fortunately, another RNZAF Kittyhawk followed him all the way down, weaving as he went, and the Zeros broke off the engagement and disappeared. George released his parachute just before hitting the water when he inflated his Mae West and then his dinghy.

As he sat in the dinghy he tried to keep it in the same position, using a hand paddle, in the knowledge that the pilot who had followed him down would report his position. He was wearing his flying suit over shirt and shorts and he carried a revolver, ammunition and a jungle knife.

After some four hours in the dinghy, George spotted four Zeros about five miles distant, flying in from the north at about 2,000 feet. He abandoned the dinghy and swam about twenty yards away. However, the Zeros passed overhead without given any signs of having seen him, and later turned back towards Kahili. George then tried to swim back to the dinghy, but the current was carrying it inshore towards Mono Island. To make life easier he decided to jettison his revolver, boots and belt, but kept the knife in the leg pocket of his flying suit.

Supported only by his Mae West, George remained in the water until dusk. The water temperature was pleasantly warm and he saw no sign of sharks. As the light faded he stripped off everything except singlet and underpants, removed his arms from the Mae West and tied it tightly around his chest. Then began a long and exhausting swim towards the mouth of the Soanatalu river on Mono Island, which he finally reached after dark. Then he curled up on the beach and went to sleep.

Waking at sunrise, he found himself on a sandy strip of beach at the mouth of the river. A coconut discovered on the beach provided breakfast. Then he decided to head west towards what appeared to be dense jungle. Before starting out, however, he ripped the lifejacket and removed the kapok lining, which he wrapped around his feet and bound in place with the fabric.

He climbed a ridge above the shoreline and headed west through broken jungle. It was imperative that he contact the natives. The Intelligence Officer had also warned that the south coast of the island was occupied by Japanese. Throughout the whole of that first day he saw no one, nor did he find any food. Water, however, was plentiful, provided by small streams running down from the hills. Flies were very troublesome during the day, especially around his feet, but disappeared at nightfall. He was not bothered by mosquitoes and for a second night he slept soundly.

He continued next day in a westerly direction, moving around the foot of the hills which covered the centre of the island. Since the previous day he had eaten nothing, and among all the varieties of the island's exotic vegetation he could not recognize any of the fruit-bearing trees illustrated in the pilot's manual. It was early afternoon when he was brought to an abrupt halt: about half-a-mile away, dressed in khaki and carrying rifles, were three Japanese soldiers, apparently on routine patrol.

George did not wait to find out whether he had been spotted; he disappeared into the jungle and headed for the hills. Then his luck changed. Where the jungle was less dense he found more coconuts and assuaged his hunger with the meat, washed down with the milk.

For some days he remained in the central part of the island, lost among the hills. Plenty more coconuts became available, but they lacked nourishment and George found himself getting gradually weaker, although he remained reasonably fit and did not suffer from dysentery. His constant aim was to return to the coast. For several more days he plodded on, until eventually he was rewarded by the sight of the ocean. His relief was tempered by the realization that he had finished up only a short distance from his original starting point.

This time he trudged along the shoreline in an easterly direction. Four days elapsed as he became increasingly exhausted, staggering along the beach like a drunken man. But determination eventually brought its reward. He suddenly found himself in a small village, consisting of only two huts, and was confronted by a party of natives, four men and four women. By this time he could barely walk. The natives carried him into the village and fed him with a boiled egg and some cooked roots – not unlike potato, but very stringy and indigestible. They were very friendly and spoke broken English, taught by Australian Methodist missionaries who had a church on the south coast of the island. It was thirty-two days since George's ditching.

They decided to hide him in the jungle so that he would not be discovered by the Japanese, who they described as 'demon men'. They built a lean-to shelter of stakes and branches and brought him some hot water and lemons, the juice of which he squeezed into the water for a thirst-quenching drink.

On the following day he was feeling considerably better after a good night's sleep in the village. That evening he was strapped across an outrigger canoe by two of the natives and taken to a place on the eastern tip of the island. The small party spent the night in a cave.

Next morning, 27 October, the sound of heavy explosions was music to George's ears, as the south coast of the island was bombarded by a force of American destroyers. With the four natives he headed overland back to the original village, but he was still very weak and was carried by his companions for most of the journey. He was overjoyed to find that Mono Island had now been invaded by New Zealand troops. He was examined by an officer of the N.Z. Medical Corps before being put on a landing craft the next day and taken to a field hospital which the New Zealanders had set up on neighbouring Sterling Island. He remained there for six days and was then evacuated to Guadalcanal.

Looking back today on his remarkable experience, George Luoni recalls that he did augment his monotonous diet of coconut with the raw meat of an occasional land-crab, which he would kill with a stick or stone. He also caught some small fish, similar to sardines, and also ate them raw. Only a few days after landing on the island, his home-made sandals fell to bits and his feet were cut quite badly by the coral as he tramped along the beach. The biggest mistake he made, George says, was to throw away his jungle knife when he discarded his clothes in the water.

Anyone who may have been dreaming of escaping from modern civilization and spending some time in the tranquillity of a desert island should reconsider their ambitions in the light of this story of a Second World War Robinson Crusoe.

BACK WET FROM NÜRNBERG

Second World War historians are generally agreed that Bomber Command's raid on Nürnberg on the night of 30 March, 1944, was an unmitigated disaster. It is believed that more RAF aircrews were lost that night than on any other bombing mission during the war. The events of that dramatic night have already been well documented, notably by Martin Middlebrook in *The Nürnberg Raid*.

One of the aircraft that managed to avoid destruction over Germany was a Mark III Halifax of 429 Squadron, operating from RAF Leeming, and piloted by Flying Officer Jim Wilson of the Royal Canadian Air Force. His rear gunner that night was Douglas Finlay, a Flight Lieutenant from New Zealand. They had bombed the target and were homeward bound when they were attacked by a night fighter in the region of Stuttgart. The Halifax was heavily damaged but not disabled, but the navigator, Cyril Way, was wounded in the leg. Field dressings were applied to the wound by the wireless operator, Stan Sharp. The Halifax struggled on towards the French coast.

During the attack the aircraft's compass had been put out of action and the pilot could only maintain the course for base with the aid of fixes obtained by Stan Sharp. As they reached the coast near Le Havre, however, the fuel tanks were found to be almost empty. The wireless operator sent out an SOS and the crew assumed ditching positions.

On the impact of ditching the Halifax broke in two fore and aft of the wings and the main spar. The dinghy was released, but had been damaged; only half of it inflated. As the crew climbed out on to the wing of the aircraft they found themselves one member short. Jim Wilson, the pilot, was missing. Stan Sharp went back into the fuselage, only to discover that the nose section of the Halifax had broken away completely. There was no sign of Jim.

The remaining crew members finally assembled in the floating half of the dinghy and pulled the damaged part over their legs to keep out as much water as possible. Five of them sat round the edge, while the wounded navigator was able to lie in the well of the dinghy.

Some five hours later, on the morning of 31 March, the Halifax crew were spotted by two fighter aircraft; one flew low over the dinghy, while the other climbed in order to transmit the position. Then came two Air Sea Rescue seaplanes. Both attempted a landing on the water, but the sea was far too rough and the attempt was abandoned. They dropped two dinghies to the unfortunate crew, but both landed on the wrong side of them and drifted away.

After another anxious period of waiting and hoping, the Halifax crew were finally rescued by ASR launches based at Newhaven. First aboard was the wounded navigator, soon joined by his companions. Together they welcomed a change of clothing and some hot soup. They had been adrift in the Channel for ten hours.

On their return to Leeming by train, Stan Sharp and Doug Finlay were both wearing survival gear – battle dress, white aircrew sweaters, overcoats and Wellingtons. They were unshaven and decidedly scruffy. Sitting opposite in the compartment was an elderly gentleman who asked if they were merchant seamen. When they told him they were RAF, says Doug Finlay, he gave them a very peculiar look and did not speak to them again.

EVEN A WALRUS CAN'T SWIM

It was not only bomber crews and fighter pilots in the Second World War who suffered the indignity of finding themselves adrift on the surface of some unfriendly sea. Those who served with the Air Sea Rescue services also had their problems, as Arnold Divers will tell you.

A pilot with the Royal New Zealand Air Force, Arnold flew the Walrus amphibious aircraft with 283 Squadron from various bases in the middle East. His first conflict with the 'drink' occurred early in July, 1943, when he took off from Maison Blanche in Algiers to rescue the crew of a Beaufighter which had been shot down two miles south of the island of Sardinia. After making a successful night landing in heavy seas and taking aboard the Beaufighter's pilot and navigator, Arnold found that it was impossible to get his Walrus airborne again. The seas were too heavy and the airframe of the Walrus had been damaged on landing. For nine hours the aircraft taxied through the swell towards North Africa until it finally ran out of fuel.

In the daylight the next morning they were able to send mirror signals to a Hudson flying overhead, which fixed their position and sent for help. This arrived in the form of High Speed Launches 176 and 182, which towed the stricken Walrus back to Bone harbour after 27 hours on the water.

Four months later Arnold had been promoted to Flight Sergeant and was operating from Palermo in Sicily. On 3 November, with his WOP/AG Sgt Keeble, he took off in his Walrus to search for the survivors of a ditched Boeing B.25 bomber of the USAAF 82 Squadron. About an hour and a half after take-off they saw a single red Very light, flew towards it and landed on the sea. The light was failing rapidly as they landed and there was a moderate swell. By the light of the Walrus's searchlight they were able to locate two dinghies, lashed together, carrying the survivors of the B.25, which had been hit by flak over the target. It had gone out of control and the crew had baled out.

When the Americans had been taken aboard the Walrus, Arnold decided to try to return to base and make a night landing. Once again, however, take-off proved to be impossible. The aircraft 'porpoised' violently across the wave caps. Moreover, its weight was now increased by the five rescued airmen. Arnold accepted the inevitable; they would have to spend the night on the water. He threw out drogues and settled down to take turns with Sgt Keeble in manning the bilge pumps.

By mid-evening the wind had increased and the sea became rougher; the Walrus began to roll heavily. The engines were started so that the aircraft's head could be kept into the wind and the buffeting reduced. As night approached, however, the Walrus began to list to port and the mainplane was under water. By midnight the list was very pronounced; the mainplane was bending under the weight of the sea and was in danger of being wrenched loose at the wing root. Arnold took turns with Sgt Keeble in climbing out on to the starboard wing to counteract the list to port, but they were only partially successful. It became obvious that the port float was damaged and had filled with water.

In the early hours of the following morning the seas were breaking right over the Walrus and the situation seemed serious. Suddenly they saw a light on the horizon, prompting them to fire two Very lights and to signal for help with the Aldis lamp. Less then an hour later the Walrus was brilliantly illuminated by a ship's searchlight and within ten minutes a motor launch had drawn alongside. The five American airmen were transferred to the launch, but Arnold and his colleague explained their intention of remaining with the Walrus in the hope of keeping it afloat until morning, when it could be taken in tow. But by this time the Walrus was virtually heeling over in the swell. The skipper of the motor launch gave Arnold an order that it be abandoned. The seas were now so heavy that the launch could no longer remain along-side the aircraft. Ropes were thrown across and the two members of the Walrus crew were half-dragged and half-swam across to the launch.

Together with the American airmen, Arnold and his colleague were put on board the hospital ship *Seminole* and taken to Naples. The ship's master gave them a written statement that he had taken the seven men aboard because in his judgment the Walrus would not have survived the night.

The Walrus crew were little the worse for their adventure, although it is worth mentioning that Arnold Divers had flown the rescue sortie only because no other pilots were available at the time, and that he was then convalescing from an attack of malaria. Surely, not the recommended treatment for a speedy recovery!

On 8 March, 1944, Arnold was in trouble again. It was reported that a Spitfire pilot had baled out north of Elba, so at 0845 Arnold (now a Warrant Officer) took off in his Walrus to effect yet another rescue. On this occasion all appeared to go well. It was daylight, the ditched pilot was located and collected, and the Walrus became airborne again without difficulty. Arnold set course for base in Corsica.

Suddenly there was an explosion as the Walrus was hit by flak. As he landed once more on the water, Arnold's aircraft was ablaze; fortunately the three men escaped and boarded the dinghy. For the next four hours, however, they became the target for 88 mm and 105 mm enemy guns on shore, until they were eventually rescued by High Speed Launch 2543 and taken back to Corsica. Members of the launch crew were later awarded the DSC and DCM for effecting the rescue under heavy fire.

IT WAS NICE FLOATING DOWN

The Cockney expression 'a load of old cobblers' had an abbreviated equivalent among RAF aircrews: they referred simply to 'duff gen': a succinct translation of false information. It was responsible for all manner of disasters.

In May, 1943, Mark V Spitfires of 485 New Zealand Squadron were being used to test a new radar technique which was supposed to give more accurate information on the positions and height of enemy aircraft. Flying with his Squadron on an offensive sweep over France at 20,000 feet, John Pattison heard that there was a large formation of Focke-Wulf 190s some 10,000 feet below. Duff gen! They were, in fact, 10,000 feet above the Spitfires and flying out of the sun. The Germans attacked with gusto and there was a loud bang as John's engine was shot away and his cockpit filled rapidly with white glycol smoke.

Surprisingly, John found himself unhurt. After a struggle he managed to open the cockpit hood, turned the oxygen on fully and made a Mayday distress call. In reply he received a course back to base and a request to make a final call before baling out. The engineless Spitfire glided down in a straight line, fortunately not seen by the triumphant enemy who had already disposed of four Spitfires, until at about 2,000 feet John made his last call to base ('It looks bloody cold down there'), unplugged his radio and turned his useless aircraft upside down. He was shot from the cockpit like a bullet from a gun. He pulled his ripcord and as he floated down towards the water he discarded his helmet and flying boots, which seemed to float gracefully above him as his descent was faster. Just before he hit the sea he released his parachute, held his nose, looked at his watch and regretted that his parachute descent had not lasted longer – he had found it most enjoyable. He struggled aboard the inflating dinghy.

A lone Spitfire flying back to base spotted the dinghy, much to John's relief. He had already seen an ASR rescue launch from Dover collect another member of the Squadron – one who had been dragged under the water by his parachute and drowned. Some two hours after ditching, John was hauled aboard a rescue launch and offered a beer glass full of neat rum. He had been so seasick that he could not accept it. 'Bad luck,' said the skipper of the launch, as he downed it himself.

As a postscript to this story, John tells us that his future wife at that time, a WAAF, was on duty as a plotter in the operations room that afternoon.

PASS THE PORT

A Fleet Air Arm shore-based pilot attached to a fleet requirements unit operating from the Royal Naval Air Station at Dekheila, on the outskirts of Alexandria harbour, Lieutenant Commander Murray Wilson was waiting for a passage back home to New Zealand in June, 1944, for his 'foreign service' leave. He had a right royal send-off.

On 21 June he was flying his Mark II Defiant, with his air gunner, on exercises with the British cruiser HMS *Birmingham*, sailing through the Mediterranean to Gibraltar. On the way back to base the Defiant had an engine failure. This aircraft had a large 'scoop' radiator on the underside of the fuselage which made it very dangerous to ditch. There was every chance that it would turn straight over on to its back, giving the crew little hope of survival.

The two men baled out of the crippled aircraft and Murray scrambled into his 'K' type one-man dinghy. The air gunner had landed some distance away. Fortunately, it was noticed on the *Birmingham* that the plane had disappeared off their radar screen, and, after checking with Murray's base, the ship turned about and steamed back on their expected track. The two airmen were located; a whaler was lowered from the *Birmingham* and they were taken aboard. Meanwhile, however, the Air Sea Rescue service had been quick off the mark. They collected Murray and his gunner from the cruiser and took them back to base in Alexandria harbour.

They were a little disconcerted to find that at the base all officers were attending a formal dinner in honour of a visit from their Group Captain, Max Aitken, son of Lord Beaverbrook, later to become a Member of Parliament. Murray and his companion were persuaded to take their places at the dinner table. They made an odd couple, sitting there in survival gear of boiler suits and seamen's boots. Murray's air gunner, moreover, was not commissioned and was most concerned about how he should behave. Murray told him to do exactly as the others did – pass the port, but in no circumstances put it down on the table.

The two airmen were eventually delivered back to Dekheila at about midnight, rather the worse for wear – socially, that is.

CHIT-CHAT IN THE CARIBBEAN

No sea is a friendly sea when one is dropped into it unintentionally. We have heard about the hazards of the North Sea and the English Channel, often bitterly cold and rough, and the vastness of the Pacific. Jack Sisley from Auckland, a Fleet Air Arm pilot in the Second World War, can disillusion the many tourists who extol the delights of yet another stretch of water – the Caribbean.

At about ten o'clock on 12 April, 1944, on a blue, tropical morning, a Grumman Goose aircraft plunged into the sunlit water some ten miles from the coast of Trinidad. The pilot and joy-riding co-pilot, neither of whom had buckled their seat belts, were thrown clear when the cockpit was wrenched from the fuselage on impact. The observer and wireless operator escaped through a rear hatch. The wrecked aircraft sank swiftly, taking the dinghy with it to the sea bed. The four airmen had only two Mae Wests between them. They shed their flying boots and leather jackets and huddled together for mutual support against the surging waves and possible attack from sharks or barracudas. Jack maintains that the cakes of anti-shark dye were most effective, so much so that for several years after the event each crewman was stained a light coffee colour which allowed them the status of 'honorary Creole'.

The wireless operator had been badly injured, having almost scalped himself on the instrument panel. His hair was first tied back on to the scalp with a handkerchief, after which he was given a shot of morphine. He slumped into a restless sleep and took no part in the next phase of survival, which by common agreement was to keep talking.

Cricket was the first topic, as the pilot, co-pilot and observer were all keen fans or players. The New Zealand and West Indian teams were analysed in depth. Discussion then passed on to those

136

games which had been played in the West Indian villages, often on coconut matting laid on unprepared turf, when batsmen risked life and limb from the thunderbolts hurled down by budding Constantines. But the risks were well rewarded in the after-match functions, when gracious Creole hosts plied the cricketers with rum and ginger, fearfully hot curries, luscious fruits and impromptu calypso sessions. As the four airmen huddled together in the water, the conversation turned to the diversity of the entertainment on the station at Piarco, Trinidad, with memorable performances by such world-famous stars as the Andrews Sisters, Lawrence Tibbett, Winifred Attwell, Yehudi Menuhin and many others.

Their reminiscences were suddenly interrupted as the wireless operator leaned sideways and vomited. 'Just what we need,' someone commented, 'ground bait for the bloody sharks.' Soon, however, the discussion was resumed: which was the best place to go on leave? The unanimous choice was Barbados, where every able-bodied male appeared to have rushed off to defend King George, leaving the womenfolk behind to be placated by any strangers who happened to stumble upon their plight in that island paradise. Perhaps the fact that it was now well after lunch-time prompted some grumbling about the lucky Yanks at Chaguaramas, the US naval base, which was rich in all those things that Piarco seemed to lack: T-bone steaks, potatoes, coca-cola machines, water fountains, a juke box and a spacious, comfortable mess. The base, adjacent to Port of Spain, had been carved out of jungle swamp on a 99-year lease to the Americans, in return for a few ancient destroyers for Britain.

There was also the recollection of an exotic meal made from a giant iguana which had strayed into the station. An interested group watched as the mess cooks slaughtered the creature with the blow of an axe and later served iguana soup and meat that looked and tasted like veal.

'By the way,' said the pilot, now confidently treading water, 'how do we account for the presence of an unauthorised co-pilot on this trip?' Jack said he had merely accepted the pilot's invitation to 'come along for the ride' because his own Albacore flight had been cancelled. The pilot's momentary anxiety was later justified: the Court of Inquiry into the loss of the Grumman revealed that the pilot had flown less than 10 hours solo on that type of aircraft. The result? A logbook endorsement and loss of seniority, leaving Jack to sing, 'You'll get no promotion this side of the ocean . . .'

Rescue and relief arrived at last in the form of a motor launch from Port of Spain. Urgent arms heaved the waterlogged bodies aboard. Stripped of remaining underwear, each man was wrapped in blankets for the homeward journey. Offers of sweet tea and cigarettes were followed by retching as salt water was disgorged from lungs and stomachs. At the dockside stretcher bearers removed the quartet to a nearby Naval hospital. A doctor, dispensing bucolic humour, had a sewing session on various lacerations and, finally, after saying, 'This may sting a little', proceeded to cauterize the wounds by pouring raw alcohol on them. The language was unrepeatable.

Alone in bed, waiting for sleep, Jack recalled a magic moment that would remain in the memory down the years. When the aircraft hit the water the pilot, of solid Yorkshire descent, was one of those without a Mae West. As he floundered in the sea he was yelling, 'I can't swim – I can't swim!' Floating nearby in his Mae West, Jack had called back, 'We're only ten miles from land, so it's a bloody good opportunity to learn!'

FLOATING KIWIS

Ditchings during the Second World War were commonplace, when damaged aircraft returning from action over enemy territory were forced to splash down in one sea or another. In peacetime, however, it is not unknown for aircraft to suffer the same fate.

A former navigator of the Royal New Zealand Air Force, Ken Thorn, tells the story of his own ditching in October, 1952. A Royal Naval 'T' class submarine was exercising with Catalina crews of the RNZAF based at Lauthala Bay, a few miles east of Suva. Catalina search radar was by no means 'state of the art' and the use of the Mark 1 'eyeball' was used in early exercises for the purpose of detecting periscope and schnorkel waves from a height of about 1,000 feet. Members of RN submarine crews were often carried on some of these flights to give them an idea of the difficulties faced by aircrew.

Shortly after arriving on station, Ken's aircraft suffered a severe internal haemorrhage of the port engine, probably caused by a conrod piercing a cylinder head. There was a loud explosion and all the oil in that engine escaped into the atmosphere in a very short time, producing a smoke-like plume from the nacelle, a rapid rise in temperature and a healthy glow inside the nacelle, clearly visible from the navigator's station in the aircraft. A secondary effect was a rise in Ken's pulse rate when the Flight Engineer announced on the intercom that they had a possible engine fire.

The pilot's notes for this type of emergency called for an immediate landing and, since compliance with the notes avoided a heap of paperwork and a greater likelihood of continued employment for the captain, he carried out a rapid descent to the nearest stretch of the Pacific, about a thousand feet away, with scant regard for the Squadron's aircraft strength. At the time, the Catalina was probably within gliding range of Lauthala Bay, but in the heat of the moment – and the heat of the engine – strict compliance with the rules was the order of the day. It is also worth reporting that the pilot, Squadron Leader S. O. Field, was also the Squadron's Commanding Officer.

In defiance of all odds, the crew prepared in the brief time available for an open-sea landing outside Suva harbour, where the water was some 300 fathoms deep. Fortunately the weather was fine with a light breeze of about 15 knots. The remaining engine was being operated at almost full power, as the complete loss of oil had prevented the port engine from being feathered. At about 500 feet Ken advised the pilot that there was no sign of fire (there had never been any flames, simply a bright red glow), but he either ignored the report or failed to hear the call. Only the radio operator was with Ken in the crew compartment, and from his seat Ken was able to give his colleagues a warning before touch-down.

On impact with the water control was lost almost immediately as the Catalina cavorted through a 360 degree landing run which resulted in at least a dozen contacts with the water. Several parts of the aircraft, such as floats and ailerons, were left behind in huge flurries of spray. During this uncontrollable charge across the ocean Ken and the radio operator were taking rather a pounding in the crew compartment. Eventually Ken's seat support sheared off and he finished up on his back beneath the radio station. The radio operator managed to remain in his seat, but suffered some back injuries.

When the rampaging Catalina ran out of inertia it came to a halt minus both floats, both ailerons and with a tear in the hull just aft of the navigator's station. The forward port strut supporting the mainplane had torn free when the port wingtip made heavy contact with the water. As luck would have it, there were no disabling injuries to crew or passengers and the evacuation was begun without delay from the two rear gun blisters, thanks to two very experienced crew members stationed there. Most of the occupants boarded the liferafts in that area. The co-pilot came back through the cockpit bulkhead, saw that the crew were attempting their escape, realized that he could go no farther aft and so escaped through the hatch above the cockpit. From there he walked along the submerged mainplane and boarded one of the liferafts.

Meanwhile, back in the navigation department, all was not going well. The water rose rapidly over the table as the Catalina sank by the nose and the radio operator had difficulty in freeing himself because of his back injuries. Ken was able to free the jammed hatch above the table and help his colleague out of the aircraft, but by the time this was done Ken found he had to swim to the surface, helped by a quick, firm tug on the Mae West inflation toggle and a rather selfish desire not to go down with the ship.

The dinghies were still close by and they were soon dragged aboard. This was shark territory, but the survivors had no time to think about it until later. There had been radio contact with Lauthala Bay tower and other aircraft had been circling the crippled Catalina. A high-speed launch was despatched at full speed, but the effort was such a shock to one of the vessel's engines that it developed a fault surprisingly similar to that which brought about the demise of the Catalina's port engine. Other squadron aircraft were monitoring the Catalina's progress, but, having seen its arrival in the open sea, they apparently decided that there had been enough Squadron heroes created that day, and possibly the thought of all the extra paperwork generated by another débâcle had deterred them from doing anything more than showing their presence in the area and taking photos of the proceedings for the subsequent Court of Inquiry. One very alert crew member deserved full marks for filming the entire sequence, from the first appearance of 'smoke' to the rather unusual method of dousing any fire, and the rescue of the Catalina's crew.

They were put ashore on Suva Wharf and met by the Station Commander, Medical Officer, Marine Warrant Officer, Transport Officer and a few Squadron members. There were also some very confused Fijians who did not know the origins of the motley bunch.

There were a few other aspects of the incident which Ken Thorn has recalled. In a later discussion with the three RN submariners he got the distinct impression that they had envisaged an earlier-than-planned return to their submarine; they had also commented on the possibility of the submarine popping up between the dinghies. The Catalina's Flight Engineer, a man of above-average height and generous build, had surprised everyone by escaping from the engineer's 'tower', complete with Mae West, through a very small hatch beneath the mainplane. It was not the sort of

action he could be expected to practise on a regular basis, but no
doubt the motivation level on that occasion was very high.

Catalina crew:
Pilot: Squadron Leader S. O. Field
Co-pilot: Flying Officer R. R. Black
Navigator: Ken Thorn
Signallers: F/Lt B. J. T. Heath, M/S M. Gartrells
             and Sgt N. J. Crump
Flight Eng.: M/E L. G. Woods

A NASTY LITTLE BUOY

One of the more recent peacetime ditchings was that of Captain Clive Plane, who was a Contract Officer with the Abu Dhabi Air Force Transport Command from 1972 to 1977. He flew the Lake Amphibian, Islander and Caribou aircraft. After completing five years' service he left the Abu Dhabi Air Force and joined Gulf Air, returning home to New Zealand in 1980.

27 January, 1976, was a perfect day to practise circuits and landings in Crown Prince Khalifa's Lake Amphibian, with clear skies and a light breeze ruffling the surface of the practice water strip adjacent to the airfield. He signed the authorization book, grabbed a Mae West and headed off for an hour's 'jolly'. Unknown to Clive, something nasty lay in wait for him.

Right in the middle of the practice strip, invisible just below the surface of the water, floated a large steel sphere: his own personal 'watcher buoy'. These large steel buoys were used to support heavy dredging pipes. As they lost their buoyancy they were discarded and allowed to sink to the bottom. Some of them, however, refused to sink and drifted for weeks below the surface before they finally settled in the mud. These rogues were known as 'watcher buoys'.

Clive met his watcher buoy at the end of his second take-off run. The aircraft ricocheted off the buoy and dived nose first into the water. The force of the water smashed the windshield and slammed Clive back into the cabin of the aircraft, seat and all.

When he regained his senses he found himself under water. The aircraft was inverted, with Clive still strapped to the seat which was no longer attached to the floor. He quickly released his seat belt, swam up the cabin and scrambled out through the hole which had previously been the windshield. Breathing the fresh air, he clambered up on to the upturned hull to take stock. He found he was minus Mae West, shoes and headset, but at least he was conveniently within sight of the airfield's control tower.

Air Traffic Control had immediately contacted the Abu Dhabi operations centre, but unfortunately for Clive most of the air and land forces were involved in desert manoeuvres on that day, including the duty helicopter rescue crew. Very unusual circumstances, of course, but simply Sod's Law in action.

After the initial shock had worn off, Clive felt rather battered and sore. Blood was oozing from a gash on his head, he had cracked ribs and general cuts and bruises. He was certainly in no fit state to swim ashore, even if he had been so inclined; sharks were not unknown in those waters.

Clearly there was only one thing to do: he sat on the hull to await rescue and waved to the air traffic control staff.

Suddenly a hissing sound alerted him to the fact that air was escaping from the damaged hull and the aircraft would soon disappear beneath the water. Sure enough, it did. Clive decided to strip off his clothes and float on his back until rescue arrived. In a moment of mental brilliance he tucked his car keys into his underpants so that he could drive home after he reached the shore.

After drifting for about forty minutes, the combined effects of shock, injuries and the mid-winter Gulf temperatures created symptoms of fairly severe hypothermia. Clive found himself hallucinating badly, drifting in and out of consciousness and getting rather fed up with life in general. At last a Puma aircraft with a Pakistani crew arrived on the scene and a very large and very welcome Sudanese crewman was winched down to rescue Clive by the 'mutual hug' method. Clive gave three silent cheers for the United Nations. The embrace was broken as they reached the inside of the Puma. Clive collapsed, rolled across the cabin and almost fell out of the opposite door back into the sea.

There was a quick flight back to base and a stretcher ride to the sick bay to be transferred to the capable hands of the Air Force's Lebanese doctor. Clive's temperature failed to register on the thermometer and rapid body warming methods were employed: towels were wrapped around his ankles and near-boiling water poured over them, while a blow heater was turned on beneath the blanket in which Clive was loosely wrapped. Feeling eventually began to return and he began shivering violently, 'nearly shaking the sick bay off its foundations'. This was the welcome return to the land of the living.

His car keys were not needed after all. He was driven home by his friend the doctor and met by his wife Doreen, who had been vaguely advised of his unauthorized swim.

BIRTH OF THE RESCUE CRAFT

In 1931 a member of the Royal Air Force with the lowest of service rank witnessed a flying boat crash on landing. It convinced him of the need for rescue craft, and he subsequently became totally involved in the testing of high-speed tenders which had just been commissioned by the RAF. The man's name was Aircraftsman Shaw, more widely known as Lawrence of Arabia.

In about 1934 the Air Ministry placed an order with the British Powerboat Company of Hythe to design and build a prototype Air Sea Rescue launch. The result was RAF 100, a fast 64-foot launch powered by three Napier aircraft engines adapted for marine salt water cooling and capable of speeds in excess of 40 mph.

On 26 May, 1936, HSL 100 made a non-stop run from Grimsby to Hythe on the Solent, a distance of 373 miles, at an average speed of 36.2 mph, a record at that time.

A further seven craft were ordered and these became the nucleus of what was to become the largest Air Sea Rescue group in the world. By the end of the Second World War these launches and their RAF crews saved over 13,000 aircrew and others from a watery grave, operating wherever the RAF was operating. Most of these wonderful launches have been lost for ever, but one or two are still around, mainly converted to houseboats.

One of those 37-foot high-speed tenders with which Aircraftsman Shaw was involved, No.206, has recently been restored by Phillip Clabburn, a 28-year-old civil engineer from Sevenhampton, who has so far spent over £25,000 of his own money in returning 206 to its former glory. He has also taken on the task of restoring a former High Speed Launch, HSL 102, to its original condition. This 64-foot launch, built in 1936, was the third

146

launch taken 'on charge' by the RAF, the first two being 100 and 101.

HSL 102 has been bought by Phillip and was brought round to the dock at Fawley Power Station, then lifted on to a cradle on land and prepared for restoration. Careful work has already been started on 102; every section of the superstructure has been removed and set aside for repair and restoration, every plank has been lifted, inspected and stacked for possible re-use. Every brass screw in the hull – there were thousands – has been removed, and all bulkheads have been repaired and strengthened. Each screw is replaced in epoxy resin. A great polythene tent was erected over the boat so that work could continue through the Winter.

New engines worth £70,000 were offered by Cummins Engineering, the successors to Napier Engines. Various engineering departments at universities and technical colleges volunteered to reproduce those parts of the superstructure which were beyond repair. REME at Marchwood donated a lot of timber, as did the Southampton Timber Company. Almost every supplier is charging only at cost. Fawley Power Station not only lent the site, but also buildings, workshops, storage, etc.

Some wonderful voluntary work has been done by ex-ships' carpenters and technicians who had served on these boats, and the young members of the Air Training Corps helped every week on the less technical jobs. They listened in awe to the tales of the older helpers. One young lady said, 'Oh, it's great – I'm working on history.'

Phillip Clabburn hoped to have the launch ready for early 1996. Then he could emulate the 1936 feat with a run from Hythe to Bristol to join the Bristol International Festival of the Sea, being held at that port in May, 1996.

The Air Sea Rescue and Marine Craft Sections Club is an organization formed by those who served on RAF Marine Craft and are supporting the great work being done by Phillip by helping him financially to re-create a vital part of the Air Sea Rescue Service. The Club sponsored the laying of the main deck and is hoping to raise sufficient money to assist Phillip in the cost of restoration. It is intended to include on the deck a brass plaque devoted to all those supporting the venture.

Ultimately it is planned to use the boat to re-live history, so that both young and old can experience the excitement of such a superb craft.

(Reproduced by courtesy of the A.S.R./M.C.S. Club)

MIND THOSE MINES

Martin A. Smith of Mattapoisett, Massachusetts, USA, was the tail gunner in a B.17 from 452 Bomber Group returning from a raid on a synthetic oil plant at Brux in Czechoslovakia on the afternoon of 12 May, 1944.

After being attacked by ME 109s over Chemnitz, a third engine failed and the aircraft eventually ditched in the Channel off Gravelines. The pilot of a P.47 Thunderbolt fighter circled above the bomber, dived towards them and dropped one of his gloves. This was found to contain a note assuring the crew that a rescue vessel was in sight.

The crew of the Air Sea Rescue craft which finally collected all ten crew members of the B.17 (two of whom were wounded) complained mildly that the bomber had managed to ditch success- fully right in the middle of a minefield. The bomber crew, however, were delighted to discover that the rescue craft carried a couple of bottles of brandy (contrary to the practice of the US Navy, appar- ently) and these were duly despatched on the return journey to Ramsgate. There were also some tins of soup which were heated by the simple expedient of punching a hole in the bottom of the can, so exposing some chemicals to the air.

Before boarding one of the two rubber dinghies, Martin had been in the water supported by his Mae West. On the rescue craft he stripped off his soaking clothes and covered his nakedness with a raincoat and a pair of rubber boots, taken from supplies on the vessel. He ended up walking from the dock at Ramsgate clutching the front panels of the raincoat together to avoid frightening the onlookers.

Two other bombers were known to have ditched in the Channel that afternoon; one came down very close to the French coast and was fired on from the shore until the crew were rescued by a Walrus. The other ditched closer to England and the crew were also picked up by an Air Sea Rescue craft.

Martin's luck ran out not long after this incident, when his aircraft was shot down over France and he was captured by the Germans and spent the remainder of the war in Stalag Luft IV and Stalag 357 at Fallingbostel.

COMPASSION

Many strange things happen in wartime and often go unrecorded. Here is one of them. It has nothing to do with ditching, but it is such a vivid illustration of one man's humanity towards another that it is worth telling.

Charles L. Brown, commander, and his ten-man crew were flying a B.17 Flying Fortress on 20 December, 1943, attacking targets in the Bremen area. His squadron, the 379th Bomb Group, were attacked by fifteen ME 109 fighters during an engagement lasting about twenty minutes.

When the fighters withdrew, Charlie Brown's aircraft had three of its four engines shot out, the entire left stabilizer and ninety per cent of the rudder were gone, the nose had been shot off and the instruments were useless. The rear gunner was dead and four other crew members, including Brown, were wounded.

With only one engine still operating, Brown coaxed the B.17 along at 200 feet. As he passed over a German air base at Jever, First Lieutenant and Squadron Commander Franz Stigler, aged 26, was refuelling his ME 109. He had already shot down two bombers in that day's engagement. Seeing the damaged B.17 over the airfield, Stigler scrambled back into his fighter and took off in pursuit.

'I went after him to shoot him down. I had all my guns ready and my fingers on the trigger,' Stigler recalls. 'I was waiting for the rear gunner to shoot, but he didn't, so I came closer and closer. There was a big hole in the back. The window was shot away, and I saw him lying there, bleeding profusely, so I couldn't shoot him.'

Moving forwards to the front of the bomber, he drew level with Charlie Brown. Realizing the complete helplessness of the American crew, Stigler saluted his enemy pilot. 'When he saw me, he almost fell out of the chair. He couldn't believe I was there. I waved at him again, and he looked again. Finally he understood that I didn't want to do him any harm.'

In a CBC interview in 1992, Brown said, 'We were looking at each other eyeball to eyeball. In all the training, there had never been anything to tell you what to do when a German fighter is flying formation with you.'

The German pilot guided the crippled bomber between two islands and two flak batteries. Charlie Brown and his remaining crew limped on over the English Channel at 200 feet and eventually the B.17 crash-landed at their own aerodrome.

Charlie Brown survived the war and told his story to fellow Legion members in Florida. Regrettably, they didn't believe him, so he spent the ensuing five years writing letters in an attempt to substantiate his report. He finally contacted the German Fighter Pilots' Association, which published his enquiry in their magazine. His letter produced a reply from none other than Franz Stigler himself, who had also survived the war and had emigrated to Canada in 1953, to settle in Surrey in the province of British Columbia.

The two veterans met in Seattle in 1989. 'We had a nice time in Seattle,' said Stigler. 'We got a little drunk.' Both men are now in their seventies and have become good friends, conversing by 'phone nearly every week and meeting twice a year.

Stigler answered the crucial question: why did he not shoot down Charlie and his crew? After all, he was a very successful fighter pilot with 28 confirmed kills to his credit at the end of the war. 'I saw him lying there bleeding. Of course I couldn't shoot him. I waved to them and guided them overseas,' he said in the CBC interview. 'I saw the guy's eyes; I had just come out of fierce combat. I just couldn't. I saw that man – I couldn't shoot that man.'

Stigler had naturally kept very quiet for years about his action. 'If it had been reported he would have been tried, court-martialled and shot,' said Brown. He added that if Stigler *had* completed his third kill that day, 'he would have received an automatic Knight's Cross, Germany's highest decoration'.

In 1993 the compassion shown by Stigler, the much-decorated fighter pilot who survived 400 combat missions, was finally recognized. In November he received the following letter from the *Fédération des Combattants Alliés en Europe* (F.C.A.E.E.):

'I have recently been in communication with a new member of the F.C.A.E.E., Charles L. Brown of Miami, Florida, and he has made me aware of the incident which took place in the skies over Germany and the adjacent seas on December 20, 1943.

'An act of chivalry and humanitarianism, such as the one you carried out in ensuring the safe return of the B.17 U.S. bomber "Ye Olde Pub", is one which should not go unrecognised, even fifty years after the incident.

'I am pleased to inform you that the Western Canada Section of the F.C.A.E.E. has approved the award of the Commander grade of the Order of the Star of Peace to you "in recognition of merit and devotion to the cause of justice and understanding for Peace in the World".'

War historian and Langley businessman George Brown presented Stigler with the award on behalf of the F.C.A.E.E. 'I think the story is absolutely incredible,' he said. 'It's amazing that both these guys survived the war and it's even more amazing that they found each other.'

Charlie Brown was unfortunately unable to attend the presentation, but he called Stigler on the fiftieth anniversary of their first meeting. Stigler, for his part, said he was happy to see Brown alive. 'It was worth it to risk a court martial, or whatever.'

HERE COMES THE NAVY!

On the evening of 14 November, 1940, Flying Officer Jack Marshall from Christchurch in New Zealand took off in a Wellington bomber for Berlin. There were six in the crew: the captain was Sergeant Morson (known to all as 'Swede'), Sergeant 'Dixie' Dean was co-pilot, George Bury the observer, 'Clev' Cleverley the wireless operator and 'Gin' Iles the front gunner. Jack was in the rear turret.

The outward trip was uneventful and the target was bombed at about 9.15 p.m. The Huns made great efforts to knock them out of the sky, but without success. So, still intact, the 'Wimpey' headed for home.

On the return course they passed east of Hamburg, where the anti-aircraft fire was very intense, and soon after they crossed the coast, flew out to sea for about three miles and then turned to fly level with the Dutch coast. It was then that 'Swede' noticed that the oil gauge for the starboard engine was registering nil and that the temperature was rising fast. Shortly afterwards the engine spluttered and caught fire.

As rear gunner, sitting in splendid isolation in the tail, Jack decided it was time to find out what was happening. He opened his turret doors and the first thing he saw was George Bury struggling with the fire extinguisher, which he soon put into operation; the extinguisher itself was mounted inside the engine cowling and very soon the fire was put out, leaving the starboard engine dead.

But the crew's troubles were by no means over. It was discovered that the oil feed to the port engine was not effective and it was necessary to put the hand pump into action. 'Sod's Law' imposed itself when the pump handle broke off about three inches from its base. As a result, Jack found himself lying on his back beside another crew member, pushing and pulling on the stump of the handle in an effort to provide the remaining engine with the necessary oil. It was extremely hard work and both crewmen broke into a sweat, even though the temperature in the aircraft was 15 degrees below zero. Nevertheless they continued their efforts, with the aim of keeping up the pressure in the supply pipe. Then the oil ran out; shortly afterwards so did the petrol.

From the time the fire broke out in the starboard engine until the fuel ran out, other crew members had been busy jettisoning all excess weight – ammunition, guns, oxygen bottles. Everything which would be no use in the immediate future was thrown overboard. They also rid themselves of all their flying kit except parachute harnesses and Mae Wests, which they partially inflated. Then there was nothing left to do but to take up their positions on the floor and brace themselves for the moment they hit the sea.

The Wellington hit the waves at about 3.15 a.m. with a terrific crash, giving the impression that it was going to dive straight to the ocean bed. Four of the crew climbed through the astro hatch, with Jack the last to go. He was surprised to find, as he emerged, that the others had already got the dinghy afloat, and all except the second pilot were seated in it. The dinghy had been carried by a wave several yards from the aircraft and Jack had visions of it drifting farther away. He plunged into the sea, which was very rough, and lashed out for the dinghy. As he was hauled aboard and regained his breath, he heard someone say, 'Poor old Dixie. He must be caught up in the aerial or something.'

The Wellington had settled on an even keel, and as Jack screwed himself round to look at it he could just make out a form hanging on to the front turret. After perhaps ten seconds the form disappeared beneath the waves, never to be seen again.

The sea was now smashing the dinghy against the aircraft. Tired as they were, the crew fought like demons to stop the dinghy from being burst by the pounding. On one rebound the dinghy came into contact with the sharp edge of a jutting piece of metal, which ripped its side like a razor. But for the fact that it had a double skin, that would have been the end of the story. Eventually the crew managed to put some distance between themselves and the Wellington and began to drift around in the North Sea, waiting for daylight. Many times during the night they heard the noise of returning bombers. They fired Very cartridges in the hope of attracting attention but with no success.

At last the sun made a welcome appearance over the horizon and the warmth of its rays was much appreciated. The sea had become quieter by about 7.15 a.m., by which time all the crew were feeling hungry, but it had been decided earlier not to break into the rations until it became really necessary. However, after struggling with many knots on the packaging, the rum was reached and distributed. Jack's first swallow, while producing welcome internal warmth, made him very sick. Swede, Clev and Gin kept it down, although they had been very ill during the night. They were all worried about George Bury, who had been coughing blood almost from the moment of boarding the dinghy.

For three more hours they drifted aimlessly until at last they spotted what they though to be a lightship. In the excitement they began paddling frantically, but after an exhausting hour the ship appeared no nearer and soon after they had to abandon their efforts. In utter exhaustion, although sleep was impossible, they tried to doze. Suddenly they heard the welcome drone of an aircraft, growing louder by the minute; it was a Wellington. With feverish haste a Very cartridge was prepared for firing, to be discharged only when the plane was as near as possible. After many hours with only the noise of the sea to be heard, the explosion of the Very pistol was ear-splitting. But the Wellington continued on its course and disappeared from sight.

The disconsolate crew decided to make one more attempt at paddling. As they began the aircraft engine was heard again. 'They're coming back!' Sure enough, the Wellington passed right overhead, as two more Very cartridges were fired directly at it. This time the signal was received. The plane flew low over the dinghy and then began circling.

Jack says it is impossible to convey the feelings he had when this occurred. They covered the whole gamut of emotions: laughter, tears of relief, intense gratitude, joy – every known sensation ran riot within him.

For three hours the Wellington continued to circle over the dinghy until it was relieved by another. By 4.30 p.m. the sun had dipped below the horizon and the sea became rougher in a freshening wind. An hour later two more aircraft joined the party, and finally in the fading light of early evening the masts of several trawlers became visible and the hopes of the crew in the dinghy rose considerably. Soon they would be on a more solid base than rubber and more comfortable than they had been for many hours. In the dinghy they had been forced to sit in the same position all the time; the result had been severe attacks of cramp. Any attempt to stretch one's legs would have caused the dinghy to capsize.

As the trawlers approached, the last of the Very cartridges was fired to guide them towards the dinghy. Then one of the two marine flares was used, with the other being held in reserve until the trawlers were so close that they could not fail to see it. It was lit as the rescue trawler, HMS *Pelton*, was just a hundred yards away. A searchlight was turned on to the sea. Jack and his companions shouted madly until a few minutes later the dinghy was bouncing against the trawler's rope ladders.

Jack took hold of one ladder but was too weak to climb; he remembers being hauled over the side by two members of the trawler's crew. Then he was below decks with a lighted cigarette in one hand and a tot of rum in the other. When the blood was recirculating again in their bodies, they stripped off their wet clothing and changed into something dry. Two buckets of hot water were provided and after a welcome wash-down they were made comfortable in ship's bunks.

The sea was again very angry and the ship was tossing in what, to landlubbers, was an alarming manner. During the night 'action stations' was sounded, but the intruder proved to be an RAF launch sent to collect the Wellington crew. The captain of HMS *Pelton*, however, refused to hand them over for two reasons: firstly because of the very high seas then running, and secondly because he felt, correctly, that they had had enough excitement during the past twenty-four hours.

The rough weather prevented the trawler/minesweeper docking in Yarmouth until 8.30 a.m. the following day. A Naval doctor came aboard and examined Jack and his colleagues. They were then taken to Yarmouth Naval Hospital and put to bed.

It is sad to report that HMS *Pelton* was later torpedoed by a German E boat and sunk with all hands, including the skipper, J. A. Sutherland, DSC.

NO SUBSTITUTE FOR A
HONEYMOON

On the night of 11 September, 1941, Bomber Command sent 143 aircraft to various targets in north-west Germany, reporting a loss of five planes. One of these was a Whitley belonging to a group of thirty-two bombers from 4 Group, sent to attack the docks at Warnemünde. In addition, twenty Hampdens laid mines in the North Sea and the Baltic and twenty-eight aircraft attacked Channel port targets.

Two of the lost Whitleys came from 58 Squadron. One is recorded as having been 'abandoned over Harrogate while lost and low on fuel on return from Warnemünde: crashed beside the Majestic Hotel.'

Fred Bowen was the navigator on a 58 Squadron Whitley, GE-B, captained by Colin Browne; the aircraft inevitably became known as the 'Browne Bomber'. On 7 August, 1941, their Whitley was commandeered by the Flight Commander, Squadron Leader Middleton, for a trip to the 'big city' (Berlin). It returned, as Colin put it, 'looking like a kitchen colander'. When the maximum effort was called for on 11 September, Colin and Fred were allocated an older Whitley, then mainly used for ferry work and not a patch on their superbly maintained 'Browne Bomber' with its special trimmer tabs to increase manoeuvrability.

The crew on that occasion was completed by Pilot Officer R. T. White, second pilot (on his first operation), Sergeant Alex Goss, wireless operator, and a very experienced air gunner, Sergeant Jack Overson. The operation was intended to create fires in the timber yards at Warnemünde docks, and for this purpose their bomb load consisted mainly of incendiaries, plus the odd high-explosive bomb for good measure.

Colin and his crew took off from Linton-on-Ouse just before

nine o'clock that night and flew across the North Sea, with brilliant moonlight reflecting off the scattered cloud beneath. At 18,500 feet the outside temperature was minus 40 degrees Centigrade. Soon after one o'clock on 12 September the Whitley was on the run-up to the target. Colin Browne had begun the hourly routine (as required by the 'latest instructions to pilots') of successively putting the two Exactor pitch controls into fully coarse and then fine pitch, before returning to cruising pitch. Fred Bowen knew from experience that if there was any water in the hydraulic fluid, and the temperature was low enough, the water would flash-freeze, leaving the propellor stuck in an inconvenient pitch until warmer air was reached and the fluid was unfrozen.

As Colin began his routine, Fred's attention was attracted by a few bursts of flak. Coincidentally, at that moment the water in the starboard hydraulics flash-froze with the propellor in the fully coarse position. Immediately after, the engine burst into flames.

Colin reached for the fire extinguisher button close to his left elbow, but failed to find it. Both Fred and the second pilot confirmed later that the two buttons were missing from their normal position. Clearly someone had blundered. Fred gave Colin a course for the first leg back to base, and on the turn Colin managed to dowse the flames by performing a violent sideslip. The Whitley was losing height at about 500 feet per minute, but this was soon doubled by the drag of the dead propellor. In those days the propellor of a Whitley could not be fully feathered. Colin re-started the engine in the hope of altering the pitch and reducing the drag, but it flamed once more and had to be switched off. This time the fire died of its own accord. By now the crew realized that they had little chance of making it back to England, so Fred gave his captain a course for Sweden and the crew set about the task of jettisoning all the non-essential gear in the aircraft.

P. O. White went through the procedure for getting rid of the forward hatch, situated at the bottom of the well leading to the bomb sight and front gun (later events showed that it had merely opened). Fred passed him various items to dump, including the astrograph, flare pistol, cartridges, navigation instruments and so on. Meanwhile Alex Goss was busy informing base of their predicament; his signals, incidentally, were received by a New Zealander, Sergeant Norman Bidwell, who was on watch that night and who the crew would later meet in a German prison camp. The signal acknowledged, Alex screwed down his key in the hope that a fix could be taken on the Whitley; then he began passing up his loose gear for jettisoning. The bomb load had already been released by Colin, but without being armed from the switch in the bomb sight. At the tail end Jack Overson was dumping photo flares before returning to his turret to get rid of the guns and ammunition.

The noise made by all the loose gear hurtling earthwards may have resulted in the frightening fan of tracer fire from ground batteries which zipped around the Whitley as Jack returned to his turret. He had just moved his head backwards when a couple of shells ripped through the bottom of the turret and out again past his left eye without exploding.

By this time the Whitley was down to 1,500 feet and hopes of reaching Sweden were rapidly disappearing. At 800 feet Colin still had no idea whether he could 'belly-flop' or ditch. At 400 feet a row of tall trees loomed ahead at right angles to their course; with little hope of clearing them, Colin spotted the glint of water, managed a reasonably gentle turn to port and levelled out before splashing down into the Baltic between two islands which were later discovered to be Lolland and Falster.

Pilot Officer White was thrown into the well on impact and went feet first through the wooden hatch cover; this time, fortunately, it broke away. The only way for him to go was down, but outside the aircraft he found he was still anchored by his oxygen feed-pipe. Ripping off his mask, he reached the leading edge of the starboard wing, quite exhausted and desperately gasping for air. Jack was out of his turret when the aircraft struck the water and was flung along the fuselage, hitting his head and back. Nevertheless, he set about releasing the dinghy from the mid-fuselage door. Of the remaining three in the cabin, Colin went out of the roof hatch above his pilot's position, followed by Fred with a hefty heave from Alex. Jack was yelling for help with the dinghy which, as so often happened, had inflated upside down. It was soon realized that it could not be inverted, so Jack manoeuvred it round to the starboard wing. Alex was ranting and raving inside the fuselage about his frustrated honeymoon. Colin and Fred heaved P/O White into the dinghy and Alex was finally persuaded to join his companions from the fast-sinking Whitley. As the dinghy was pushed off GE-D sank beneath the waves with its landing lights still blazing.

The night was calm, but the survivors were not. P/O White was still waterlogged; no one relished the idea of taking to the water to reverse the dinghy, so they sat smoking and bemoaning their fate. Alex still complained about his lost honeymoon and the fact that he had entrusted £50 to his room mate; P/O White had lost his lucky rabbit's foot, while Colin ascribed their disaster to the fact that he had forgotten to don his 'lucky flying stockings' and had only recently bought himself a Colt 45 revolver, which had gone down with the aircraft. Moreover, he mentioned bitterly that his tour of operations would have finished if he had got back to England. Fred confessed to having felt edgy before take-off, but merely sat on the upturned dinghy eating the rice-paper flimsies with secret data.

After a while, efforts were made to paddle the dinghy towards land, but they were of little use and the dinghy was still quite close to the point of ditching when it was sighted by one of a fleet of five Danish fishing boats sailing in 'V' formation and carrying German naval ratings. The captain of one of the boats warned the crew, in English, to dump any secret information they were carrying. Colin and his colleagues had no choice but to be taken aboard while the Germans, with some difficulty, hauled in the dinghy. Jack reached for the knife attached to it and tried to rip the rubber, but was frustrated by his captors. He then quietly suggested to Fred that they could take on the German ratings and sail off to Sweden. Fred pointed out that the ratings on the other boats, now circling the rescue vessel, might react in a hostile manner. According to Colin Browne, a wide circle of luminescence was still filtering up from the Whitley's landing lights, so it could not have been in water too deep for the Germans to have salvaged it.

The crew were herded below decks, where the Danes introduced them to acorn coffee and said that their names would be passed on to England. They had been moored at the far end of one of the islands and were ordered by the Germans to search for survivors. Taken by the Germans to Nykobing, the crew went from there by truck to a Luftwaffe station near Vordingborg and spent the night after being interrogated by their hosts in the usual way. Later a ferry took them to Warnemünde, to be transferred to a train for the journey to Dulag Luft, the Luftwaffe interrrogation centre at Oberursel near Frankfurt, and thence into captivity for the rest of the war.

The late Colin Browne, who was secretary of the Goldfish Club for many years until his death in 1985, added his own reminiscence to the story of his ditching:

'One thing I shall never forget is sitting in the back of a troop transport lorry, surrounded by a bunch of German soldiers who insisted on singing gleefully, "We're going to hang out the washing on the Siegfried Line". You could say it was a bit of a come-down!'

WHAT ELSE CAN HAPPEN?

It is an indisputable fact that the fate of many bomber crews in the Second World War was determined by circumstances which were totally unpredictable. One Halifax bomber of 420 (Royal Canadian Air Force) Squadron which attacked Kiel in September, 1944, should never have taken off from its airfield in Yorkshire. The crew, captained by Flight Lieutenant V. T. Motherwell, were officially on stand-by but were called in at the last moment because of illness among members of another crew. The air bomber and navigator, Alastair MacDonald, also revealed that the Halifax was comparatively new to the Squadron, and its two previous attempts to take part in operations had been aborted because of the malfunction of equipment.

En route to Kiel Alastair discovered that the direct compass was out of action and the flight had to be made on the magnetic compass. Flying over the North Sea, the bomber's 'Gee' radar system also became partly disabled; in order to maintain his 'blip' on the screen, Alastair was obliged to jiggle the antenna continuously. By the time they had reached the Danish coast, they were flying by map reading. The North Sea had been crossed at only 2,000 feet; there was heavy cloud from that level up to a height of 20,000 feet, and only on reaching the Danish coast was the pilot able to climb to bombing height. Alastair says that the Germans 'did a good job of lighting up the sky on the run in to Kiel' and he was able to see the target being attacked by the other bombers.

About twenty minutes after leaving Kiel things began to happen to the Halifax. First of all, one wheel came down, then the other, followed by flaps and bomb doors. The crew were not aware that the aircraft had been damaged by flak, but they had lost all the oil pressure on the hydraulics. Reaching the coast, they descended

163

once more to 2,000 feet and thus created another problem: at that height the engines overheated and it was necessary to use rich mixture fuel to keep engine temperatures within tolerable limits. It was finally realized that the fuel would be exhausted before reaching the English coast.

There was only one alternative – ditching, and with the wheels down. Fortunately the pilot managed to put the Halifax down almost in a stall, so that the belly of the plane hit the wavetops before the wheels dug into the water. As the aircraft filled rapidly, the crew escaped from their various exits and climbed into the dinghy.

By noon the next day no rescue had arrived, although aircraft had been seen on search patrols. It was decided to erect the dinghy's sail, but, with one supporting line missing and the crew's numb fingers, this operation lasted almost three hours. Moreover, the only direction in which the dinghy would be taken by the prevailing wind was back towards the coast of Europe.

At five o'clock in the afternoon three aircraft flew by close enough to the dinghy to be recognized as coming from the crew's own station. 'Anyone who has looked for dinghies in the North Sea,' commented Alastair MacDonald, 'knows that they can readily be lost from sight again. All kinds of flares were dropped around us and soon it seemed that we had an Armada of aircraft circling above, including two Walruses, two Hudsons with life-boats, and fighter aircraft.'

At 8 p.m. one of the Walruses came in for a landing, although the sea was still very rough. But the attempt was successful and the Halifax crew were taken aboard. The Walrus pilot told them that they had been waiting for an ASR launch to arrive, but as it was now getting dark they had decided not to wait any longer. If no ASR boat arrived, they would have to taxi back to the UK. Although the Halifax had ditched at a point no more than 50 miles from England, the dinghy had been carried by the wind to within thirty miles of Europe, and the Germans were well aware of their presence – hence the fighter protection.

Eventually an ASR launch did arrive on the scene and the crew were transferred. The Walrus pilot made an unsuccessful attempt to become airborne and his aircraft was taken in tow by the launch. 'Shortly thereafter,' says Alastair, 'a star shell was dropped over the boat, unbeknown to us because we had been put to sleep with pea soup and a cup of Navy rum. It was a British warship asking for identification. They then advised that all haste should be made to an English port, because German E-boats were now out chasing us.' The naval vessel gave them cover and some time after midnight the launch arrived at its base.

Next day the pilot of the Walrus called in to say farewell. His Walrus had been cut adrift and a friend of his was going to fly him out in an attempt to find it. They did – and he flew it home.

After ten days' leave, Alastair and his fellow crew members went back on operations and completed their tour.

APPENDIX 1

REUNION OF RESCUED AND RESCUERS

Tributes to the RAF Air Sea Rescue Service were paid at a reunion in Lyme Regis in 1994. About 300 guests attended a two-day reunion, organized by marine craft historian and author Ken Rimell.

The visitors came from all over the world: France, Belgium, Germany and the USA were all represented. The event was held to bring together airmen rescued from the sea by RAF marine craft during the Second World War and those who rescued them.

The reunion was well supported by former members of the RAF Marine Craft Unit at Lyme Regis, accommodated in premises now occupied by the outdoor adventure centre. It was something of a triumph for Ken Rimell, who had spent months studying old records and contacting airmen who had ended up in the water after returning from their missions.

Ken told a nostalgic gathering at the Power Boat Club that some 200 Americans had been expected to attend, but that number had been greatly reduced owing to the last-minute bankruptcy of the holiday company arranging the flights.

Included in the reunion activities were a commemoration dinner in the Power Boat Club, a service at Cobb and a 'special tribute' fly-past by aircraft en route to the Culdrose air show.

Ken was the official RAF photographer when the Lyme Regis RAF Marine Craft Unit finally closed in 1964. He said: 'This reunion is the most difficult I have organized because of the logistics involved, but it is certainly the most rewarding, especially as it is attended by men who were present when the Lyme Regis unit opened in 1937 and by others who were present at its closure.'

Among the rescued was Jim Myl, now aged 71, of Los Almitos, California. He had been the pilot of a B.17 bomber who was forced to bale out over the North Sea after an aborted raid on Munich in 1944. His full story is told on page 28. 'I guess we were about 80 miles from land when we baled out,' said Jim. 'I was in the water for over three hours before I saw an RAF rescue craft coming. Believe me, it looked like the gates of Heaven had opened for me. When I joined the Air Force in 1942 I was just 18 and had left my mum and dad behind; there was only us. I just had to come back today and say thank you, because now, when we have a party at home there are 26 people present, including my 92-year-old mother, my six children and the grandchildren.'

Among the 'ditched' contingent from Britain was Len Cullingford of Winchester, whose story also appears on page 71. He came down with his Dakota on D-Day, having been in the lead aircraft towing gliders. Len said, 'We had to release our tows from 500 feet and we were badly shot up. One engine had gone as we tried to get back and the other was pretty useless. We had to ditch in the Channel and were there about 30 minutes before being picked up. Having rescued us, the skipper of the rescue craft decided to stay the night with the invasion fleet off Normandy – and that was very scary.'

Len is now 78; he was wounded in both arms and legs during the raid and was eventually taken to Southampton hospital.

One year before the Lyme Regis reunion a commemorative plaque was unveiled on the premises formerly occupied by the Lyme Regis RAF Marine Craft Unit. The plaque had been donated by the D-Day Aviation Museum at Chichester and the unveiling ceremony was performed by Mrs Shunan Hall of Chard, whose late father, Sir Algernon Guinness, had commanded the Unit from 1942 to 1945.

APPENDIX 2

THE GOLDFISH CLUB

The Goldfish Club was founded in 1942 by Mr C. A. Robertson, who was at that time Chief Draughtsman of Messrs P. B. Cow & Co Ltd, one of the largest manufacturers of Air Sea Rescue equipment in the world. In addition, 'Robbie' was also responsible for the Ministry of Aircraft Production's Air Sea Rescue drawing office. This department (which had taken over the experimental work done by the Royal Aircraft Establishment, Farnborough) made working drawings of rubber dinghies and other Air Sea Rescue equipment made by factories in the United Kingdom, the Commonwealth and the USA.

Many ditched aircrew survivors visited the office to discuss their experiences with the equipment they had used. After hearing some of these stories, Robbie conceived the idea of forming an exclusive Club for airmen who had survived the wartime aircraft ditching and who owed their lives to the successful use of the Mae West, rubber dinghy, etc. Such a Club would, he felt, enable members to meet and exchange experiences.

With P. B. Cow's financial backing, the Club was named the Goldfish Club – gold for the value of life and fish for the sea – and a badge was designed showing a white-winged goldfish flying above two symbolic blue waves. Each member was presented with a heat-sealed waterproof membership card and an embroidered badge. Due to wartime regulations, production of wire badges was prohibited and all cloth severely rationed. However, these problems were overcome and silk embroidery substituted for wire upon black cloth cut from many evening dress suits sent by readers of the *Daily Express*, after an appeal by columnist William Hickey.

The badge was generally worn by Naval aircrews upon their Mae Wests and by the Royal Air Force crews under the flap of the left-hand battledress pocket as, due to service dress regulations, it could not be shown on the uniform.

Apart from a few announcements in advertisement columns of the aeronautical magazines, the first real article about the Club appeared in *The Aeroplane* on 26 March, 1943, written by the Editor, the late Mr Colston Shepherd. However, the spoken word was one jump ahead of the written word, as the British Broadcasting Corporation had already broadcast in January of that year from Robbie's office, when Wynford Vaughan-Thomas interviewed the founder and two members who had ditched on their first operational flight.

News of the formation of the Club spread rapidly, even into the prisoner-of-war camps where eligible aircrews soon claimed membership. Their cards and badges were usually sent to their next-of-kin for safe keeping until their escape or release.

Whilst the Air Ministry did not acknowledge the Club's existence, Squadron Adjutants very soon began to forward membership application forms from their own aircrews who had qualified. The Royal Air Force Intelligence Branch also routed some enquiries through to check that the details being given to substantiate claims did not contravene the Official Secrets Act.

In 1944 the Imperial War Museum requested specimens of the Club badge and membership card for inclusion in their section devoted to Second World War exhibits, and in 1978 they last confirmed that the items were still in good condition and shown periodically on rotation.

By the end of the war the Club had 9,000 members and it had been intended that the granting of further membership should cease. However, during the ensuing months, application forms continued arriving and it became obvious that the spirit of the Club was still very much alive. When Robbie resigned his post with P. B. Cow Ltd in September, 1947, to start business on his own account, he retained all Club records so that he could continue the administration at his own expense.

In January, 1951, Raymond Blunt, who was at the time Editor of the RAF Association Journal *Airmail*, contacted Robbie for news. As a result, he published in subsequent editions a series of articles on individual wartime ditching experiences. Many members wrote in and enquired about the possibility of a reunion dinner.

With this encouragement, Robbie and Raymond Blunt organised the first dinner at The White House Restaurant in Alley Street, London N.W.1. on 26 May, 1951, and this received wide publicity in many national newspapers and magazines. The dinner was an unqualified success and it was decided there and then to reorganize the Club upon a permanent basis, managed by a committee which was finally elected on 6 March, 1953. The Reunion Dinners have been held annually ever since, at varying venues with many distinguished guests.

In the early days of the formation of the Club, and by kind permission of the RAF Reserves Club, 14 South Street, London W1, the Club was allowed to use their premises as a London address, and committee meetings were held there until that Club closed in 1970. Meetings were also held at the RNVR Club in Hill Street and at the Pathfinder Club in Mount Street, until the Club moved into the premises of the Sesame Club, Grosvenor Street. For the past few years the Club has been meeting at the Polish Air Force Club near Earl's Court.

In 1955 eight epic stories were gathered together and published under the title *Down in the Drink*. The Club's insignia has been embroidered on to ties, woven into cravats and ties, printed on Christmas cards, cast into horse bronzes and emblazoned on cuff links, lapel badges and car badges.

*   *   *

While this book was in preparation the authors learned with deep regret of the death of the Club's founder, Mr C.A. Robertson.

INDEX

Figures in italics refer to the plates

115,	103	420 (RCAF),	163
145,	52	427 (RCAF),	54
207,	97	429,	127
216,	38	432 (RCAF),	120
249,	52	452 (USAAF),	149
280,	81	485 (NZ),	132
281,	81	486,	23
283,	129	489 (NZ),	49
340 (USAAF),	99	501,	44
355 (USAAF),	33	511 (USAAF),	28
379 (USAAF),	151	512,	71
402 (RCAF),	42	514,	46
403,	54	617,	*22, 23, 24*
419 (RCAF),	76	619,	95